Library of Congress Control Number: 2001098720

ISBN 1-58150-075-0

Printed in Hong Kong
Second Edition: October 2002

Distributed to the trade by
National Book Network
4720-A Boston Way
Lanham, MD 20706
1.800.462.6420

a division of The Blood-Horse, Inc.
PUBLISHERS SINCE 1916

ECLIPSE
PRESS

RIDE OF THEIR LIVES

The Triumphs and Turmoil of Today's Top Jockeys

LENNY SHULMAN

Foreword by
TOM HAMMOND

ECLIPSE
PRESS

Lexington, Kentucky

Dedicated to my Dad,
who got me started in this game;
and to Neil Lustig,
who kept me going in it.

Contents

Foreword

As I travel the world for NBC sports, I encounter dozens of talented athletes. But none intrigue me more than jockeys. Small in stature, large in heart, they put their lives on the line in every race.

The successful jockey must possess strength, excellent eye-hand coordination, steely nerve, a sense of time and pace, and the ability to communicate with his equine partner. And all these attributes must be contained in a body that falls within the weight limits required by racing. Imagine a football player having to weigh in before the game, then being told he was too heavy to play.

The weight issue adds a unique element to the jockey's career. Where many sports put a premium on athletes attaining great size, the jockey must stay within a rigid framework of allowable weight while maintaining the same athletic qualities as his larger contemporaries. Riders sometimes go to extreme measures to maintain optimum weight. More than once I have seen a jockey finish a full meal, head to the restroom, and "flip," or regurgitate, his food.

I believe this obsession with weight can affect jockeys in a variety of negative ways. Constant dieting may leave them so weak they are unable to control their mounts, endangering themselves and their fellow riders. It may cloud their decision-making process, dulling their senses. In the extreme, it can lead to self-destructive and erratic behavior, perhaps even drug and alcohol abuse.

Thankfully, increased knowledge of nutrition has enabled the modern jockey to escape many of the horrors of the past. Though the weight requirements remain in place, several states have revised their scale of weights upward.

Despite these daunting job requirements, there are those who stand out in their profession. The elite riders have their own signature. Jerry Bailey is the ultimate big race jockey. Pat Day is able to communicate with his mounts, urging them to relax. For a complete horseman, try Chris McCarron. Jorge Chavez had the inner strength to fight his way out of poverty. Laffit Pincay has tremendous physical strength; Gary Stevens incredible determination and tolerance for pain; and Eddie Delahoussaye legendary patience. The life stories of these and other jockeys detailed in *Ride of Their Lives* tell us how their personalities were shaped and their abilities honed.

The public generally discounts jockeys as true athletes. To the contrary, I believe the best jockeys are among the most gifted of athletic performers.

These are individuals small in stature but giants in their sport.

— *Tom Hammond*

Introduction

At every racetrack across the country there is an easy-to-miss, nondescript door, like a secret portal behind a living-room bookcase. At some tracks it is just off the saddling paddock, at others in the middle of a dank tunnel or around a corner and up a flight of stairs. A uniformed officer usually lurks in the portal's shadow. Every thirty minutes, foot traffic flows in and out. Outbound, the room's residents emerge wrapped in clean silk, heads held high and hopes intact. To me, each horse race officially begins when that door opens and the parade of jockeys marches toward their mounts.

Inbound, post-race, the riders peel off muddy clothes and discard loosened bandages and unrealized dreams. Entering the sanctuary that is the jockeys' room is to be greeted by organized chaos. A sea of small men (and women in separate quarters) wearing sleeveless undershirts and white riding pants dart about, their heavily muscled arms the only clue that you're in the presence of athletes.

A television set is often tuned to a daytime soap, or, on the weekends, to a golf tournament or football game. Golf is popular among riders, most of whom play on their days off. Someone holds up his football betting card, comparing his choices to the scores streaming across the bottom of the screen. Someone else stares at the TV, looking right through it.

The pool table is unused, with balls strewn aimlessly across the felt. A card game breaks out around a makeshift table of crates, its players tossing cards about, none of them paying attention.

Over in the corner a rider is on the phone desperately trying to make last-minute travel changes. A jockey and his agent erupt in a screaming match. Some riders clip clop to the steam box to "pull" a couple of pounds. Others head to the omnipresent food counter, always thick with activity despite riders' constant battle to lose or at least maintain weight. Energy has to come from somewhere.

There are, in descending order of usage, cigarettes, Bibles, and Stairmasters. Sometimes it's so quiet you can hear a pound drop; other times it's rowdy as a frat house. All jockeys but one will be losers after any given race. It is no shock then that fistfights become a regular part of the scene.

These, after all, are competitors. They've always had to be. As kids they were smaller and lighter than their classmates. Most became wrestlers in school because they were athletic, and it was the only sport in which they could compete against their peers. Dreams of professional careers in football, basketball, and baseball were crushed by lack of size. Riding became the outlet for their competitive thirst.

These jockeys grew up farm boys and cowboys and

tough guys, from the bayous of Louisiana to the buttes of Colorado and New Mexico to the mean streets of poverty in Central America and South America. Their families usually owned horses or trained them, and the future jocks, for the most part, got a leg up at a tender age.

With their futures mapped out by the time puberty arrived, too many dropped out of school. Early success as a rider frequently turned out to be a curse. The combustible combination of too much money and not enough maturity and education led many to the barroom and the cocaine straw, where they became fighters and addicts. And if the money and the unsavory characters they collected didn't lead them to drugs, the constant struggle to reduce weight often did.

They are charged with controlling unpredictable animals twelve times their weight, and many do so without the benefit of proper nutrition or a clear head. It is not too dramatic to say they put their lives and well being on the line each time they ride onto a racetrack. For this, they are rewarded with catcalls and jeers from a crowd allowed to assemble mere feet away. Usually a crowd that is upset at having less money than it possessed thirty minutes before.

The elite few are well paid. The overwhelming majority toil anonymously on minor-circuit tracks, plying their trade on freezing nights for consumers who care nothing for them unless they manage to return a few bucks, and even then they are forgotten as soon as the next race goes off. Or strictly for the love of the horse and of riding, they wake before dawn to work, for little money, as exercise riders in the mornings. They climb on and off horses, hoping to gain the confidence of an owner or trainer who will offer them a mount in a race.

On horseback they are at home. Adjusting a stirrup or knotting up a rein, they give the appearance, sometimes an illusion, of being in control. On foot, parading out of the jocks' room single file toward the paddock, whips in hand, dressed regally in colorful silks of the moneyed owners, they are a collective force, a huge part of the pomp and circumstance that is horse racing.

But when you see them walking through an airport, for instance, you realize their isolation as individuals, as complete as a seven-foot-tall basketball player's. Then, you can begin to understand the fire that burns within them to fit in, or to excel, or to fight for their turf.

The riders profiled herein are among the lucky few and have reached a high measure of success in their trade. Success has not come cheaply.

Most have emerged from the other end of their hell-raising days as likable and compassionate people. There is little in any of them that suggests the separation common between big-time athletes and their fans. The ones I have spent time with, or merely observed, are unfailingly gracious in posing for a photo or signing an autograph. Perhaps because this game has no long-term contracts they can afford to torch few bridges.

Their lives are not presented here in search of sympathy, or to make excuses as to why they are who they are. Their stories are given in the spirit of explanation, and because they so often contain the twists and turns that make the mystery of all our lives so fascinating.

Lenny Shulman
Nonesuch, Kentucky
November 2001

1

CHRIS ANTLEY

Charismatic

No loved one should have to endure the scene that Bryan Antley found December 3, 2000, when he entered his brother's California home.

The million-dollar house outside Los Angeles was in disarray. Cryptic writing, like graffiti, littered the walls. A bedroom door was pulled off its hinges. Bedding and clothes were strewn about. Splotches of blood marred the floor and walls. And Bryan's older brother, jockey Chris Antley, lay lifeless in a hallway, a pool of blood forming a halo from a cut on his forehead.

Pasadena police were called to the scene, and they listed the cause of death as "severe trauma to the head." Paramedics termed the circumstances "suspicious," and police began a homicide investigation while the Los Angeles County Coroner's Office started its work.

Chris Antley the jockey hadn't an enemy in the world. Routinely he would peel off bills from his pocket to backstretch workers in need. Strangers whom he befriended on airplanes felt within minutes they'd known him all their lives, lauded his kindness, and recalled the instant affection they felt toward him.

But Antley, a rider possessed of divine talent, was cut down by human imperfection. In the throes of manic depression, one thinks he can befriend anyone and do anything. The bizarre actions that take hold can include associating with unsavory characters.

One such character, whom Antley met through a shared taste for methamphetamine, was arrested on unrelated drug charges shortly after Antley's death. Police, though, couldn't build a homicide case that stuck. And six weeks later when the coroner's office came forward with its findings, the jockey's death was ruled accidental and self-inflicted, caused by a lethal combination of four drugs, including amphetamines, antidepressants, and anti-seizure medication.

The investigation was closed, but the acute sense of loss remains painful to the world of horse racing, a world that Antley enriched with his winning personality and stark riding skill.

When Chris Antley died, various trainers, jockeys, agents, owners, and media members expressed grief, and sorrow rushed from each and every one's lips. What was disquieting, however, aside from the terrible loss, was the resigned acceptance that accompanied the death of the thirty-four-year-old. Nobody seemed all that surprised.

The roller-coaster ride that was Chris Antley's life had long ago left watchers gripping the handrails with white knuckles, wondering what sideways veer or topsy-turvy dip or vertical climb was next. The great triumphs and precipitous descents had already taken the breath away from observers. His professional soap opera spanned eighteen years and starred both random acts of startling kindness and grievous ones of self-destruction. Chris Antley's smooth control on the back of a horse could not have been further from the jarring, lurching ride of his life.

Horsemen always commented about what a natural Antley was on a horse. That naturalness came not from an innate skill, but from hard, concentrated work. Antley wasn't born into racing. He was born into a family that moved from Florida to Elloree, South Carolina, when he was seven. That family, however, broke up, and his parents separated shortly after Chris became a teenager. His father, an oil-company worker, moved to Columbia, an hour away.

"His family was busting up, and Chris and his younger brother and sister were having problems with that," said Franklin Smith, who trained, and still trains, horses in Elloree. "My neighbor here next to the training center had a fish pond, and Chris would go over there and fish, and I think he came out here on his bike one day looking for something to take his mind off everything else. Man, he took to the horses right off. After the first day he came out here; as soon as school was out, here he'd come."

"I was trying to be a football player," said Antley during an interview in early 2000. "But I weighed seventy-five pounds. If I weighed the same as the other guys, nobody could have handled me. At school I really wanted to fit in. You need that status. You need that Izod shirt. But I was little, and my family didn't have a lot of money."

So along with mowing lawns, Chris Antley worked at the stables, mucking stalls, pulling the manure cart, raking the shed rows, and cleaning the feed tubs. After two days, he was handed a twenty-dollar bill, and it felt pretty good to him. He could get that shirt, go out on a weekend night like the other kids who were more secure financially. He also had a purpose. He was involved with something.

At first he knew nothing about horses. He didn't even think about getting on one. He had no idea that jockeys were small. "I'd never seen racing. When the Kentucky Derby came on TV, I'd turn the channel. I had no interest at all."

At fifteen Antley began to turn horses out to pasture and bring them in. Cowboys showed him how to walk a horse around in circles. He got on yearlings, lying on their backs as they were turned in their stalls. He began shed row walking. "Some of the people here told him he looked like a jock, that he'd make a good jock," Smith said, "and it started fascinating him. Next thing you know, he was going around the barn on an old lead pony, and from then on you couldn't keep him off a horse." He was learning as the yearlings were. A cowboy taught him how to blow the horn to post through the side of his mouth. He started jogging horses. Then he tried galloping.

"The first time I galloped on the racetrack I was sitting down and hanging on to the reins," Antley said. "The other guys were standing up in the saddle, so I decided I was going to stand up. I let the reins drop loose a little, went three strides, the horse slammed on the brakes, dropped his head, and I hit the ground. My first case of humility. I had to learn. I made sure I was ready next time, and I don't remember getting dropped after that on the farm.

"In later years the word 'natural' came up a lot; people would say that about me. But as far as me knowing that, no, I was just trying to do what the other guys were doing. Everyone was caught up in which horses they were getting on and whose was better. That was the big thing: 'He got one over there that can fly.' I got on this one horse — the sign in his stall read 'Parade of Stars.' Turns out that was his father's name, but I didn't know that. He was a chestnut, and I fell in love with him."

If the horse was lying down when Antley got there after school, Chris would lie on the horse's stomach. When it was brush-up time, "Parade of Stars" was groomed until he glowed. Without a shank, the horse followed Antley around like a pony. A powerful bond formed. Antley ordered a gold riding helmet with stars around it — a parade of stars.

"With his family situation, it was a tough adjustment for a kid that age," said Smith. "What Chris was doing out here was something for him to focus on and get his mind off the other. Once he started to get involved he emptied himself out to it. He was as quick a study on a horse as anyone you could find."

His helmet arrived in time for Chris to wear for the Elloree Trials, in which he rode "Parade of Stars." The pair ended up winning the trials. After that event, the horses are up to running three-eighths of a mile, and it's time for them to ship north to the races. "When it was time for him to leave I couldn't take it," Antley said. "I put his bandages on and led him to the van. I'd bought a Ford Escort, and I followed that van up into North Carolina. It was killing me. I finally turned around three-quarters of the way through North Carolina and went back home.

"I went straight to my room and started packing an old army trunk. My mom came in and asked what I was doing. I said, 'I'm going north with Parade of Stars for the summer,' and she said, 'No you're not.' And I said, 'Watch.' I left. I went to Bubba Fogel's gas station on the corner, got a map, and went to Delaware Park."

Leaving home and high school behind, Antley headed

for the stable of Hamilton Smith, Franklin Smith's brother. Smith had no idea Antley was coming, and Antley, fifteen, could have easily passed for eight. The stable gate guard thought so too, and Antley's lack of a license ("I didn't know you needed one") got him the boot. Eventually Antley got the paperwork and began galloping horses for Hamilton Smith.

"He gave me a tough time, busted on me from the day I walked in. If I worked a horse too fast he'd say, 'Boy, take your boots off and put your tennis shoes on,' and he'd make me walk hots for a week. I'd have to rake up the walking ring when it was one hundred degrees outside. But I loved him."

Said Hamilton Smith: "I guess I was rough on him by today's standards. Like any kid he'd get to playing around and not paying attention to what he was doing, and the only way to get him to focus was to set him down. I put him on the ground for a while and he didn't like that. He'd carry on and cry. He loved getting on horses.

"He was a little baby-faced-looking thing, looked like he was about ten years old. My brother said the kid was a born natural on a racehorse, and it turned out to be. He was a good-hearted boy, do anything for anybody, hard working and conscientious about horses. Never gave me an ounce of trouble for the year I had his contract. Didn't smoke or drink at that time. Only thing that boy ever wanted to do was ride horses."

Antley began riding a race here and there, and was pulling down $117 a week at Smith's barn. Each week he'd put a hundred dollar bill under his floor mat and try to live on the seventeen dollars plus whatever he could hustle shooting pool. His chestnut love was entered in a race four weeks after Antley's arrival. He took the four crisp hundred dollar bills and bet them on the horse.

"To bet four hundred dollars on a horse…whew! But I loved this horse with a passion. And he won. I was loaded. I was The Man. They ended up running him on the grass, and he broke down. I didn't know anything about the concept of horses breaking down. I'd never seen that. But he was the horse that got me there."

The horse's real name was Surviving the Life.

Antley traveled farther north, and success followed. Just one year into his career, Antley won the first of three consecutive riding titles at Monmouth Park. At the age of twenty, he was the national leading rider in wins, scoring 469 times in 1985. Riding day and night, he triumphed in thirty-seven stakes races that year, mostly at Philadelphia Park, Monmouth Park, and Meadowlands. The following year he made the winner's circle 391 times, and in 1987, rode 340 winners. That year he became the first jockey to win nine races in a day. His name was also showing up aboard grade I victors such as Single Blade in the Gazelle Handicap, Bordeaux Bob in the Philip H. Iselin Handicap, and Without Feathers in the Monmouth Oaks. He won the latter contest again the following year with Maplejinsky.

By 1989, at age twenty-four, Antley was established in New York, becoming the leading rider there. That year he pulled a DiMaggio and won at least one race for a record sixty-four straight days. Antley was living large, but now he was living hard as well. As the eighties melted away, he had already been suspended twice for drug use. Antley's lack of education, surplus of money, battle with weight, and the proximity of unsavory company proved a prescription for disaster.

"I was young, and everything happened fast and easy for me," he said. "It was a rush to the top, with people saying 'he's great, he's this, he's that.' Now you're up in that air with all the hoopla, and by association, you're that person they're talking about. And now people are hanging around you even though you know the friendship isn't there. It wasn't like the realness of South Carolina. I'd left home when I was fifteen. I was in the big world, but I didn't know where to go. It was easy to get lost."

When Antley talked, his ice-blue eyes seemed to look straight through the listener. Nobody who saw those eyes will ever forget them, or his baby face. At age thirty-four, Antley could have passed for nineteen. "It'd be easy to say 'the racetrack is bad' or 'the racetrack has drugs and bad people who drink too much,'" he said. "But that stuff's all over the world. My faults don't come from that, they're from the process of growing up and trying to be a man of responsibility. I had to learn by being my own boss. I had money. You get a confidence of well being, but you're looking for that next outlet — whether it's to go have fun or go be depressed. It's all another vice to eliminate your feelings — be it up, down, or sideways. But it boils down to self, not the job."

The roller coaster was heading back up after Antley returned from suspension to ride the Gulfstream Park meet in 1991. There, he renewed a friendship with New York-based trainer Nick Zito. "Nicky and I had always been close," Antley said. "I'd worked a lot of horses for him, and I fit in well around his barn. We'd both been highly publicized. We clicked as a team, but it wasn't just a business relationship. We'd talk about life, too."

Zito's Strike the Gold finished a narrow second in the

ANNE M. EBERHARDT

Antley's determination earned him his second Derby.

1991 Florida Derby under Craig Perret, and was making up ground at the end of the nine furlongs. Antley got the mount on him for Keeneland's Blue Grass Stakes, and the two came away with top honors. That set up a decision for Antley, who was also the rider of the LeRoy Jolley-trained filly Meadow Star, reportedly being considered for the Kentucky Derby as well. Both trainers wanted a commitment from Antley, who had ridden Private Terms in the 1988 Derby, and Shy Tom, one year later, to off-the-board finishes.

"With two horses that looked like they could be anything, that's a hard decision," the rider said. "I talked it over with my agent, and we thought Strike the Gold's Blue Grass was tremendous. But I didn't want to go public because I wanted to stay on Meadow Star, too, and I thought they were bluffing about the Derby. So I called Nicky at home and assured him I was riding his horse, but I asked him not to make it public. The filly ended up not running in the Derby.

"There was a lot of excitement in the days before the race. Reality set in that I was going back to the Derby, and my hands were shaking when I flew into town. I'd go to Nicky's barn and stay there all day. (Trainer D. Wayne) Lukas used to laugh at me. I'd be sleeping on the bales of hay in the middle of the barn, hanging out with the help. But it made me feel like part of the team. We were a family in that stable."

Antley's biggest concern was Strike the Gold's come-from-behind running style. In a big Derby field, the trip factor looms large. "I had the confidence that we could win it, but I also felt 'just let me get lucky, let the holes open.' Those are the anxieties you get before a race like the Derby. When race time comes, there's a switch that turns off. You get into a zone where it's just another race, and people aren't hollering, and you go into a tunnel and relax. My biggest thing as a race-rider is 'don't try to make things happen.' It'll happen if you're in the right place. When you try too hard, it gets you into mistakes. You relax, get calm, and go with the horse."

As usual, Strike the Gold dropped back early, jumping up and down as he got hit with dirt kicked up by the horses in front. Antley nudged him to stay in the race and not lose position, but they sat tenth around the first turn. Antley found himself inside Angel Cordero Jr. and Quintana up the backstretch. They were both on the move, and both looking to get into a hole big enough for just one of them. Antley called Cordero "the greatest rider I ever rode with," but friendships were left at the gate.

"We're approaching that hole and Angel says to me, 'You got any horse?' 'Yeah, I got some horse, Poppy.' And just as we get to the hole, I push Angel out and he gets pinched. I angle out and the horse is running, passing horses into the turn like they're in a gallop. My rule of thumb with three-year-olds going that far is the wire's at the quarter pole. You don't close in the Derby. You stagger home.

"I had the momentum. Now I hit him left-handed, and he goes to his right lead but he's getting out. But he's still running and he's in front down the stretch. You know those security guys who stand on the outside rail without moving? They moved, 'cause I was coming straight for them. We actually went where the track was unharrowed. There were almost no pictures of that finish because the cameras weren't set that wide out. We hit the wire, and I kinda blacked out.

"I stood up and froze there at the end of the knot. When

I watch it, I get chills. I remember getting to the outrider and realizing I'd better sit down. He's galloping over to pick me up, and I'm not even trying to pull up the horse. I was in shock. During the ceremony I was like, 'Did this really happen?' Because winning the Derby is an immortal thing to any rider.

"After the Derby people would ask me who my favorite horse was, and Strike the Gold would never come up. He was an Alydar, and they're a different sort. I don't know how to say it…he was an ass. He wouldn't listen, he wouldn't pay attention, and he'd do exactly what he wanted when he wanted. He cost us the Belmont. He was much the best that day."

Antley's best was soon to desert him as well. He packed his immortality and tried to leave his East Coast troubles behind by starting fresh on the West Coast. He enjoyed solid meets in Southern California throughout 1993 and 1994, winning 204 races in '94. Solid horses such as River Flyer, Individual Style, and Stuka carried him to stakes wins. Although certainly among the top jockeys, Antley nevertheless didn't revisit his whiz kid numbers from the eighties.

By 1995 his attendance was becoming spotty. There were riding infractions and also a shoulder injury. His business slowed. The lack of a significant personal relationship weighed on him. He tired of fighting weight, and his concentration and enthusiasm for the game waned. Depression began to get the best of him, and "personal reasons" kept him off the track for part of 1996. He returned to New York briefly. Then, after accepting twenty-three mounts back at Oak Tree at Santa Anita in the autumn of 1997, he bailed out — and returned home to South Carolina.

"At this level you have to show up and play the game correctly," Antley said. "There's no slacking off. There are no contracts here. You're as good as what you've done lately. Everyone wants the hot jock. You fall off mentally. Your discipline fades over time. It's not fun anymore. You get depressed. Not all riders go through that, but I do. It would be a shock for people to go through what we do. If I could pull you through one of my bad days...you wake up six pounds too heavy and you're not excited because only half your mounts have a chance. You take water pills and coffee, depleting your vitamins and minerals. What we do to our bodies, and then go ride races. It's impossible.

"I thought my life was over at thirty. I didn't want to live anymore. It's all downhill — I'm gonna get older and uglier. It's ruin."

Around that time Antley was diagnosed with bipolar disorder, another term for manic depression, which would play all too big a role in his final years. Back in South Carolina he hit bottom, ballooning up to 147 pounds. 'What am I going to do now? What am I going to do?' he asked himself. He thought about opening a restaurant. He published a stock market newsletter via computer, but others always thought him more adept in that field than he saw himself. Finally he decided he wanted to return to riding. The roller coaster was about to make one more dramatic upward trip.

When his father left for work each morning, Antley left too. He decided that he had a job as well — to run and train and make it back to the races. "When I left the house every day, I didn't say I was going to run three or five miles. I was heading out just to put one foot in front of the other. I was geared up like Rambo. I had a ritual. All bandaged up, I'd stretch, and then head off, not knowing where I was going. I had to keep moving, and that was it. Keep moving and you don't get hungry. I'd show up at my sister's house midday and she'd make iced tea, and I'd play with her kids and shoot hoops with them; then I'd be out again.

"Go to the Wal-Mart, look at the books and magazines. I looked like a wacko. Here's this guy with a stocking cap — my Superman cap — when I put on that cap I'm The Man. I gotta have that hat, and I don't care if you look at me funny. With the Walkman and the backpack and I'm sweating — you don't see much of that in Carolina."

Antley's travels put him back in touch with reality. His runs took him past "people who didn't have jobs, kids that weren't eating. You notice a lot of things, plus the music directs you to certain areas — rebel slamming music, ghetto music, Creedence for traveling forever and not getting tired. It all made me want to get out of there. It made me want something more.

"I wish I would have taken before and after pictures. This was day and night, and not just the weight. It had to do with the soul. I had a glow in my eye. I cared about myself again. I walked into the Santa Anita jocks' room in February, 1999, at 112 pounds, and I was the fittest S.O.B. in that room by a hundred lengths. Eighteen months away. I got on horses two mornings and then I rode races."

Antley had to fight to earn his way back. Another jockey would go out of town to ride a stakes, and Antley would pick up a winning mount. Business was growing slowly, as well as could be anticipated with short fields and a dozen top riders in the room. That April he won a race for trainer D. Wayne Lukas. In the winner's circle, Lukas told Antley to watch Charismatic, who was running in the

Lexington Stakes at Keeneland the following day. "Tell me what you think," Lukas said. "He's probably going to the Derby, and you can ride him if you want."

Antley watched the race on television and got a chill inside. It wasn't the strongest field, but Charismatic, a former claiming horse, did it the right way, the same way Strike the Gold had won the Blue Grass eight years earlier. Antley figured the horse was 100-1, but it was still a chance. There were no standouts coming up to the Derby, and the possibility started building in his mind that he could actually win this thing again. He had told his dad jokingly when he left home that he was going to win the Derby. It was part of pumping himself up.

By Derby Day, Antley was talking trash to the other riders, telling them he was a cinch. Meanwhile, the first time he laid eyes on Charismatic in person was in the paddock before the Derby. He had looked over the race and strategized that he would try and stay out in the four-path rather than try to save ground down on the inside. When a horrific logjam formed down at the rail going into the Derby's first turn, it was clear Antley had made the right move. He nudged the horse to keep position the length of the backstretch. They passed a handful of horses and hit the top of the stretch behind only Cat Thief.

"Into the second turn I was still nudging, but he's slowing down a little, his legs are starting to swing, and I've already gone to the whip. But nobody's coming, and I'm thinking maybe I can stay for a piece. I kept riding hard, a steady grind. I endured him to the wire.

"I was numbed out. There was no crowd involved. It wasn't like with Strike the Gold, where you felt lucky to win a great race. This was more spiritual. The hardest dream, and it was coming true. That whole journey. I wasn't even in the game playing. And then there I was. I was so warm inside it made me cry. To get there through all that."

If Antley's victories in the Kentucky Derby and the Preakness aboard Charismatic made him an incredible comeback story, his defeat with that horse in the Belmont Stakes made him as close to a national hero as horse racing gets. He knew before the race he could be in for trouble.

"The horse was shifting and rocking in the post parade," he said. "If it wasn't for the national focus, I would have scratched him. I was scared to death, but if it's destiny that I go down…He was struggling the whole race, but he was just one of those stayers. I knew he couldn't win, and I was just giving a sigh of relief that he made it — and then it went."

Charismatic broke down in the shadow of the finish line, and Antley, reacting quickly, got off the colt's back and held his injured leg off the ground to prevent further damage. It is quite possible he saved the horse's life. On national television, more coverage was given to Charismatic post-race than to the winner, Lemon Drop Kid. In defeat, the legend of Chris Antley only grew.

"I remember walking back to the jockeys' room after the ambulance came and I'd handed Charismatic over," Antley said. "I could hear the people get louder and louder and I'm thinking the winner's galloping back awfully late. But there was no horse around. The people were yelling for me, but I'm actually still in shock. I've been involved in breakdowns, those tragedy days where you lose fifty percent of the fans. It was a miracle this wasn't one of them."

Antley seemingly couldn't lose for the remainder of the summer of 1999. He kicked home stakes winners such as

River Keen, Joe Who, A Lady From Dixie, Doneraile Court, and Forestry. But by autumn of that year he was gone once again, sidelined by a combination of balky shoulders and knees, weight problems, and depression.

There was a brief comeback at the beginning of 2000 at Santa Anita, and then the mercurial Antley left the track

MIKE CORRADO

Antley's quick reaction might have saved Charismatic.

once again — this time for good. There was hope that he would find happiness when he married ABC Sports producer Natalie Jowett in a Las Vegas ceremony in the spring. But Antley was fast becoming a recluse again. He stopped taking or returning calls from horsemen and concerned friends.

Trainer Bob Baffert, who gave the bride away at Antley's wedding, talked to him sporadically during the dramatic downward spiral that marked the last months of the rider's life. Jockey Gary Stevens visited Antley's home several times, trying to talk him into a drug rehabilitation program. He could not get through to his friend.

Anyone who has a close friend or relative mired in the throes of manic depression knows that it is, in the words of Jimi Hendrix, a "frustrating mess." You talk and talk and they seem to understand, but there is a disconnect from reality, a wild tilt between depression and mania. Things such as stress and drug use only compound the problem.

Not even the upcoming birth of his daughter could lift Antley out of his final cycle. There was a drunk-driving arrest; a methamphetamine lab in Antley's home; the destruction of computer equipment and his television; and finally, a drug overdose and a delusional fit.

"Chris may have died last week," said Baffert, "but he really left us a while ago."

The tributes poured in from all corners of the industry. Baffert called him a "fierce competitor, strong on a horse." Lukas, struggling to make sense of it all, termed him "talented, articulate, likable. He had so many plusses; it makes all of this even more of a shame."

"He always seemed to be searching for something,"

noted Gary Stevens. "Everybody has their ups and downs, and unfortunately Chris didn't respond well to the downs. He had a troubled life."

Less than a year before his death, Antley had looked forward to the future, to accomplishing more than personal triumphs. "I overcame myself this past year, and now I know I'm not done," he said. "There are other goals off away from myself. Sure, I can win the Derby again. But then it's still just you sitting there. I want to achieve something with people and learning and teaching, something that's rewarding for others. I'm tired of fighting me. That's the road I have to do."

Tragically, it is a road that will remain untraveled.

2

JERRY BAILEY

A Loner at the Top

"At the end of every year since 1990 I've said to myself, 'I don't see how it could get any better than this,' and every year it seems to get better."

There is no mistaking the speaker of these words, as for the past decade, and now into the new millennium, the name Jerry Bailey has been synonymous with winning big races. No matter if it's in Dubai or Louisville, the Triple Crown classics or the Breeders' Cup Classic, aboard the "incomparable, unbeatable" Cigar or the 133-1 impossibility Arcangues, Jerry Bailey gets to the winner's circle, time and time again.

Bailey is a fascinating study in contradictions. Whereas you can see the fire in the eyes of riders like Jorge Chavez and Gary Stevens, Bailey projects the coolness of an Aqueduct winter meeting. His post-race encounters with the media can be as warm and fuzzy as an Israeli-Palestinian negotiating session. Once engaged in conversation, though, Bailey proves to be thoughtful and intelligent.

He knows others view him as being aloof and arrogant, yet, if asked, he will help young riders on, and off, the track. He admits not socializing with any of them, yet

served hard time as president of the Jockeys' Guild and was arguably its most proactive and effective leader. Bailey is criticized frequently for taking mounts from other riders, which means simply, he is the best, the jockey whom owners and trainers want to ride in a big race. If any other riders were in the same position, they'd be doing the same thing.

If life can be lonely at the top, Bailey doesn't seem to mind. He's worked hard to get where he is, admits he is a huge overachiever, and would rather spend quiet time with his family than get involved in any racetrack hoopla anyway.

Bailey was born in 1957 in Dallas and grew up in El Paso, Texas, the son of a dentist who owned Quarter Horses and Thoroughbreds, and a mother who stressed education. "We had a pony in the yard when I was five, purchased for my older sister who showed and was an experienced rider. I rode the pony for kicks, but being a jockey was not something I was thinking about doing," Bailey said.

He wanted to be a jock, that is, an athlete, and competed in sports throughout his school years against bigger opponents. Like so many riders, he took to wrestling, the only sport in which participants take on opponents of equal weight. Bailey never got the growth spurt to compete in other contact sports. Later his smaller stature would prove a blessing, as Bailey never has had a weight problem. At age nine he began working before and after school, and in the summers, hotwalking, exercising, and grooming horses for his father's trainer. A couple of years later Bailey began spending summers at racetracks around New Mexico, and at fourteen traveled to Denver to spend the summer at the now-defunct Centennial racetrack under the guidance of J.J.

Pletcher, father of trainer Todd Pletcher. Living in the tack room of the barn there, he groomed and exercised horses.

"Once I started exercising them, I got the feel for what it was like and thought I could be a jockey. It felt good, it was fun, but I didn't have any idea if I'd be any good at it or not." One year later, at New Mexico's Sunland Park, Bailey encountered veteran jockey Ray York, who was working for Pletcher, and the journeyman gave him an education. "Ray gave me a lot of pointers," Bailey said. "He taught me to stay as close to the pace as possible without using a horse too much, and to always save something for the end." Little more than a year later, Bailey got aboard his first mount, Fetch, at Sunland Park in 1974. It should not come as a surprise that they won.

After graduating from high school in New Mexico, Bailey journeyed to the Midwest, and as an apprentice had a successful meeting at Ak-Sar-Ben in Nebraska. To broaden his interests, he took a brief hiatus to study accounting at the University of Texas at El Paso. Although he has people today who manage his money, "I'm the guy who writes the checks. Nobody else signs on the dotted line but me."

After winning the apprentice riding title at Oaklawn Park in 1976, Bailey moved up to the next level, riding in Illinois and Florida chiefly for trainer Arnold Winick. The accounting student was carefully calculating his moves up the ladder. "When I still had the bug (apprenticeship), I was offered a chance to go up to New York in 1975, but I didn't do it. I was riding in Chicago and Miami, big cities, but not New York. Then I went to New Jersey and went Jersey-Florida for a couple of years. While I was in Jersey, I would go up to New York for a race here and there, so I got a feel for it and got to know what it was like. I broke in slowly, and it wasn't as intimidating as it would have been if I'd gone to New York when I was younger."

Bailey made a big impression in his first year in the Big Apple in 1982 when he rode Copelan to grade I wins in the Champagne and the Futurity at Belmont Park, and the Hopeful at Saratoga. He was aboard a three-year-old named Fit to Fight who scored in the Jerome Handicap that year and a year later took down the Stuyvesant Handicap as well. Fit to Fight, trained by Mack Miller, and Bailey really broke through in 1984, however.

"Fit to Fight put me on the map in New York," said Bailey. "He was the first big horse I rode for (Paul Mellon's) Rokeby (Stable), and we won the handicap triple in 1984, which used to be a big thing but has gotten lost: the Metropolitan, the Brooklyn, and the Suburban. I think that gave trainers in New York more confidence in me, the fact that Mack Miller and Rokeby would ride me."

Miller, now retired and in the Racing Hall of Fame, recalled, "He came into my office and said he'd been riding in New Jersey and would like to ride a horse for me. He had his origins in the Quarter Horse business, and the first horse I put him on, the gate opened and he was six lengths in front and got beat. When he came by for coffee the next day I said, 'Hey, we have to slow this thing down a little bit.'"

Later in 1984, Bailey met his wife to be after winning Hialeah's Flamingo Stakes aboard Time for a Change, defeating Devil's Bag and Dr. Carter. Suzee Chulick, who worked for SportsChannel at the time, did a post-race interview with him. "She knew nothing about horse racing," Bailey said. "Her beat was tennis and powerboat racing, but nothing was going on that day so they sent her down to cover the horses." Today, as Bailey's wife, Suzee knows a lot more about the sport.

Bailey was clipping along steadily, if unspectacularly, in the mid-eighties, winning with fifteen percent of his mounts. He received a jolt when he walked into Miller's office one morning in 1985. "He fired me," remembered Bailey, "said he couldn't ride me on any of his horses anymore, that the decision had been made by Mr. Mellon. I was devastated. That was my main stable since 1982. I knew what it was — I had been disqualified twice on their horses in the previous six weeks, both in stakes races.

"I had just bought a new home, and I didn't think I was going to be able to survive.

"I went to work even earlier the next morning, and started riding all of John Veitch's horses for Darby Dan Farm. He gave me a tremendous boost at the time, and I survived. That firing hurt—I'd been getting on Java Gold at 5:30 every morning teaching him how to change leads and stuff, and he won the Travers the next year. But what I never quit doing was going to Mack's barn every morning and having coffee. And after a year passed, I started riding for Mack a little bit and then Rokeby, and within two years I was riding everything again and ended up winning the Derby for them in 1993 (on Sea Hero). So I've come to live by the motto that failure is not fatal and success is not final. And if you understand that, it will get you through some tough times."

The picture of stability that Bailey became in the nineties is a far cry from the personal turbulence that marked his life the previous decade. "I used to be Mr. Party Animal," he admitted. "I fell victim to the pressure and to alcohol. I was mired in mediocrity and should have been a lot better a lot earlier, but I had different priorities. I took the fun to too high a level. We haven't always been Ozzie and Harriet. When I quit drinking in 1989, my wife was on her way out the door. It was only because of her strong faith in my conviction to stop drinking that we made it.

"When I was drinking, I thought I was six-foot-eight and 240 pounds. Vincent Bracciale Jr., who rode Broad Brush, has been a good friend for years. I visited him at his farm just after I'd quit drinking, and he was making his own wine and wanted to know if I'd taste it. I told him that I'd quit. And Vinny looked at me and said, 'You know what, if anybody should have quit drinking, it was you.' He'd never said anything derogatory before about it, but that was the right perception."

For more than a dozen years now, Bailey has participated in a twelve-step program. His attitude improved vastly when he quit drinking. "My whole personality changed, as anybody's would when they stop abusing any substance," he said. "I thank a lot of the people who put up with me while I was going through all that."

Trainers tend to understand just fine when you're winning for them. "Well, he was young and single and having a good time in life," said Mack Miller. "Then he grew up, matured, and his attitude about life changed."

Continued Miller, "He always had marvelous hands, and he's a high-class fellow. He stuck with Sea Hero after the Derby when he ran a couple of bad races, then came back to win the Travers, which I grew up thinking was equally as important as the Derby. Jerry studies, he has one hell of a good mind, and he knows the strengths and weaknesses of the other horses and riders in a race. He rode most of our good ones, and a man's personality and how he conducted himself meant a lot to me."

Asked whether his riding changed when he got straight, Bailey becomes animated. "You can look at the statistics and tell me when I stopped. *You* can tell *me*. It went straight up."

Indeed, in his first full sober year, 1990, Bailey's win percentage jumped to nineteen percent and soared to twenty-four percent in graded stakes races. His stakes wins began filling up whole pages, and races like the Preakness and Belmont and Breeders' Cup Classic started popping up in his column. For the past dozen years, Bailey has been on one hellacious roll, even soaring above and beyond the handful of elite riders in his class.

"Detractors want to say, 'He gets lucky; he gets all the good horses.' That's because I work my ass off, and I pay attention," Bailey stated. "I spend a lot of hours paying attention. It's preparation and hard work, and the harder you work the luckier you get. I study each race fifteen to thirty minutes, inside and out, set up several different scenarios. If I'm not clear on it, I'll go back over it until I have a good estimation how it's going to be run. If I can't figure it out after that, I throw my hands up and just fly by the seat of my pants when I get out there.

"You have to do that once the gates open anyway, but if you're prepared for several different scenarios, you ride the race with more confidence. The guys who don't prepare, they're guessing out there when it's time to make decisions. But if you know the history of the horses and what they're likely to do, then you have an educated guess. I know when I'm sitting behind a guy who has no clue what he's doing. I handicap the riders too. I know what a rider is going to do in a situation, and I know how to react to his move because I can plan for it. And I handicap trainers as well. When you're choosing horses and they seem equal to you, you go with who you think can prepare them and get them to the race better."

Whatever his method, Bailey's results are nothing short of stunning. In 1991 he rode Hansel to victories in the Preakness and Belmont Stakes, and kicked off an incredible run of four Breeders' Cup Classic wins in five years. Legend has it that Bailey's mount in that race in 1991, Black Tie Affair, actually fell asleep in the starting gate, which the rider would neither confirm nor deny. "Well, he was very docile," Bailey allowed. "I hadn't ridden him before, and he had his head down, and there wasn't much I could do, and I was quite concerned that he may not be on top of his game when the gate opened. And then he broke like a rocket." Black Tie Affair led every step of the way.

Two years later Bailey could use little of his valued preparation when he took the Breeders' Cup Classic mount on Arcangues, a French import he had never seen. In fact, he couldn't pronounce the name, and, on top of that, couldn't find trainer Andre Fabre in the Santa Anita paddock before the race. "I didn't know what he looked like," Bailey admitted, "and now it's 'riders up' time and the grooms are speaking to me in French and I have no idea what they're talking about. I figured European style would be drop him out the back and make a run. Finally Fabre grabs me and tells me that very thing.

"Now I'm in the post parade and I look at the board and he's 99-1 (actually 133-1), and I'm thinking I hope I don't come in trailing one hundred yards behind the field. But when he broke he gave me a good feeling. I tucked him in, and with every step and every passing furlong he felt like he was running well. I had a great trip. They didn't isolate me on camera, but I felt I rode that horse every bit as good as the Sea Hero Derby and Grindstone's Derby." Indeed, Bailey moved Arcangues along the inside, split horses, and drew off by two lengths. The $269.20 mutuel is the biggest payoff in Breeders' Cup history.

A year later Bailey and Concern came storming down the Churchill Downs stretch from the clouds to nip Tabasco Cat in the Classic, and a year after that was the coronation of Cigar, the horse who cemented Bailey's place at the top of his profession, winning him the first of three consecutive Eclipse Awards and entry into the Racing Hall of Fame. In 1995 Bailey and Cigar went undefeated in ten starts, including eight grade I stakes. Ironically, for a guy who's accused

Wife Suzee and son Justin are a priority for Bailey.

of poaching mounts, Bailey inherited Cigar because Mike Smith chose to ride Devil His Due instead of the son of Palace Music in the NYRA Mile in 1994. Although Cigar lost his bid for back-to-back Breeders' Cup Classics when he fell short to Alphabet Soup in 1996, he did tie Citation's record for consecutive victories with sixteen when Bailey guided him home first in the Arlington Citation Challenge.

"It was an awesome feeling," Bailey said. "That was probably the loudest crowd he ever performed in front of.

Cigar gave Bailey some of his finest moments.

That, and when he retired and went to Madison Square Garden and it was all horse people. Those two occasions were truly amazing; very emotional." As for his biggest on-track thrills, Bailey narrowed it down to a dead heat between his first Kentucky Derby win, on Sea Hero, for Miller and Mellon, and Cigar taking the inaugural Dubai World Cup, "because it was for America. It was an Olympic-type feeling in that you're racing for more than just yourself and your horse; it's for your country."

Wherever there is a big stakes race around North America, the ubiquitous Bailey is there, likely sitting on a short-priced horse that figures to be contending at the finish. Some barns, like that of fellow Hall of Famer Bill Mott, give Bailey first call on much of their stock. "He rides whatever he wants to ride ninety-five percent of the time," said Mott. "I remember riding him in Chicago back in 1974 on a winner named Old Thunder. Then in New York around 1994 we started together in a big way. He'd ridden long enough to gain the experience to become a top rider. You have to go to war for awhile to become seasoned. Jerry works at it, he's consistent, and he zeroes in on the job at hand. He knows how the race will shape up, and he's not afraid to take a chance. He'll stay tucked in and save ground, and even though once in awhile he'll have to eat one, many times he'll get through, and that makes the difference."

Other leading trainers, such as Bobby Frankel and Bob Baffert, will ride Bailey after a horse has failed to win for another rider. Although this game of jockey musical chairs has been going on since the beginning of racing, it continues to create ill will from the jilted jockey.

In the 2001 Kentucky Derby, for instance, up-and-coming rider Victor Espinoza rode Congaree to a solid third-place finish for Baffert. He was rewarded with a pink slip before the Preakness. While Bailey picked up Congaree, Espinoza got a leg up on A P Valentine. When Espinoza's mount finished second and Bailey's third, Espinoza could barely muffle his glee.

"I don't know if being opportunistic is a good thing or a bad thing," Bailey said. "Look, I broke Gulch's maiden, and then Angel Cordero said he wanted him next time, and I never rode him again. I was the recipient of bad fortune when I started and other guys were taking my mounts, and as the circle goes around I guess it's my turn to replace other guys. Maybe before it's all over they'll be replacing me again. That's the nature of the business, and if an owner wants to change, that jock is off. I don't take it personally. Everybody's out to ride the best horse they can, and if a good horse is offered to him, he'd be a fool to turn it down.

"Occasionally you feel tension with other riders over that, sure. But I think the guys who understand the nature of the game understand it's the owner's decision who he wants on that horse. When people get uptight or jealous about me picking up good mounts, hey, I make mistakes too. I took off Go for Gin for the 1994 Kentucky Derby for Irgun, who got hurt and didn't run. I turned down the mount the next year on Thunder Gulch in the Derby."

Jockey agent Ron Anderson, who represented Gary Stevens for nearly ten years before moving on to Bailey, said, "Sure, guys get mad at you. The bottom line is every time they line up for these big races, Jerry and Gary and a few others are winning them. It wouldn't matter if they were axe murderers. As long as they're winning, nothing else matters. This is a totem pole business whether you're a jockey or an agent or a trainer. If you can knock some-body off the totem pole, you move up a rung. But don't go through a stage where you don't win or they'll forget about you in a heartbeat. There are no friends. Your friends in this business root for you to die."

If Bailey is vilified for taking, he has also given back. Bailey assumed the presidency of the Jockeys' Guild in 1989, and in his seven years in that role carried the water for several campaigns aimed at increasing rider safety. The guild persuaded tracks across the country to install safety rails to break riders' falls; it implemented the use of flak jackets, or safety vests, which are now standard equip-ment. Helmets have gotten better; and the guild persuad-ed several jurisdictions to raise the scale of weights, wide-ly considered to be better for jockeys' health. New York, New Jersey, Florida, and Kentucky have all adjusted their scales upward to varying extents.

At the end of 1994, Bailey led the guild up to an eleventh-hour strike threat when negotiations stalled between it and the Thoroughbred Racing Associations over health insurance and help for disabled riders. A strike would likely have hurt racing's already shaky image and was avoided just one day before the calendar year, and an agreement, ran out. In the end, the riders did not receive the percentage of pari-mutuel handle they sought for health insurance, settling instead for a fixed increase in benefits. The negotiations had ongoing ramifications for Bailey.

"Certain feelings were hurt, and I believe I was put on the shelf, blackballed, whatever you want to call it, for a while with a few stables. I believed in the cause so I took what came my way and kept on working. I think performance smooths over those feelings after awhile. Again, it wasn't personal. I was trying to act as a voice for the whole organization.

"In New York, the trainers get one percent of purses to fund their health insurance, and the jockeys get nothing other than what we negotiate with the TRA every year. I'd like to see jockeys get taken care of the same as the trainers. We haven't been able to do that yet. The guild has been a 'big guy helping the little guy' system for years, so the guys who have ridden a lot have been paying our own insurance, and we've actually been subsidizing the other guys and their costs, so they've gotten it very cheaply, at as little as one-third the cost. We recently reached the point where we can't continue to do that, so everybody has to pay their own way, and it hurts the little guy."

The guild suffered another painful upheaval over health insurance in 2001, underlining the importance of the issue that never was solved during or after the strike threat.

Bailey resigned the presidency in the mid-nineties so that he could spend more time at home with his young son, Justin, and because his energies were being divided. "Everything I do I do as a perfectionist, and it's very hard to be hands-on as president of the guild and still ride. It became frustrating at times because I wanted to do more and see more things through, but my time didn't allow me to do that."

Unlike other riders who suggest their touch with horses is God-given, Bailey maintains that he does not possess an abundance of natural talent. "I see guys out there who have a lot more talent than I do who achieve a lot less," he said. "I consider myself an overachiever. My success comes from hard work and preparation more than God-given talent. I didn't just luck into success."

Perhaps because of this, Bailey maintains he is always available to young riders for advice, both personal and professional. "I try to befriend young riders coming up, a responsibility I have always taken as a human being and not as a guild official or anything else. You can tell youngsters what you think they should do and what will work for them, but you can't do it for them. As far as giving away any trade secrets, I never fear that because they're the ones who have to go out and execute. And there's a very small percentage of guys coming up who want to listen anyway. Most of it falls on deaf ears. The few who are willing to listen, I'll gladly help."

It is difficult, then, to pinpoint the real Bailey. Is he the guy who poaches good horses from other riders? The veteran who is willing to give them words of wisdom? Is he unapproachable, or the man who gave tirelessly of himself for years as head of the union seeking to make life better and safer for them all? Is he aloof, or just a quiet family man? Bailey is not immune to his reputation. He makes a point of trying to explain himself. "A lot of people perceive me as being arrogant because I don't associate or socialize with a lot of the guys," he admits. "But I've been there, and my life is different now because I spend a lot of time with my family. People perceive that as being arrogant, and it's not."

Confronted by the charge that the media views him as uncooperative, Bailey tackles that perception head-on as well. There's no doubt he can blow through the assembled reporters after a race like a fullback rumbling for a key first down. "I'll be honest with you — it's very difficult because I want to win every race, and if I don't win I take it personally. And there's a certain cooling-out period — five minutes, ten minutes, where the frustration level has to drop back down again. We need some time to come back to earth, and we'll be as helpful as we can. I'll say, 'Not now.' It could mean five minutes from now, it doesn't mean 'never.'

"The competitive nature is always in me. I'm out there to win them all. I know I can't. There's eighty percent of the time when there's no reason why you should have won the race — you got outrun, there was no excuse, and you walk back as level-headed as could be. But twenty percent of the time things happen and you should have won, and in my case the adrenaline level is very high then."

As he enters his mid-forties, Bailey shows no signs of slowing down. Through the end of of 2001, his winning percentage was in the rarified air of twenty-five percent, and in graded stakes rose further still to twenty-six percent. His mounts that year earned better than twenty-two million dollars, shattering his own record set in 2000. When he was coming up, Bailey noticed that even great riders like Cordero and Jacinto Vasquez saw their business begin to slow down when they hit age forty-five. Although it would be a shock if Bailey were to retire that early, he maintains that it is a good point to evaluate where he is in terms of getting good horses and performing at a high level before assessing future plans. Being around his son more is an important consideration to him.

Perhaps Jerry Bailey is misunderstood; perhaps not. But when he is gone from the scene, racing will lose one of its more intelligent voices and a sense of humor that is often hidden from the world at large. When he won aboard the Bobby Frankel-trained Squirtle Squirt in the 2001 Breeders'

Cup Sprint, breaking Frankel's zero-for-thirty-eight drought in Breeders' Cup competition, Bailey greeted the trainer in the winner's circle with, "Fancy meeting you here."

On another occasion, Bailey remembered, "I was riding a horse at Aqueduct, for the life of me I can't remember his name, and the trainer told me he's very fast and unrateable. But he told me if I could sing to him, it might relax him. As we turned onto the backside he was rank and I couldn't slow him down or relax him, and the only song I could think of was "Jingle Bells." So I started singing "Jingle Bells" to this horse, and it actually helped. We won."

In his time, there is no one better at riding an open sleigh than Jerry Bailey.

3

RUSSELL BAZE

Just Win, Baby

I n *Casablanca,* Humphrey Bogart's Rick calls our home "this crazy, mixed-up world," and little has happened in the sixty years since to refute him. Today the straight and narrow is as unpopulated as a racetrack on a Wednesday afternoon. Normal for jockeys in our age is a background that includes one or all of the following: dropping out of school, alcohol abuse, drug abuse, diuretic abuse, starvation, purging, barroom brawls, runaway temper, domestic difficulties. Even the ones who have managed to emerge okay meandered through years of problems.

And then you ask Russell Baze to describe the biggest adversity he's had to overcome on his way to riding nearly eight thousand winners. You get a lengthy pause and then a sheepish admission. "I haven't had a whole lot of adversity," he says with a laugh. "My whole career has been pretty straight-ahead. There really haven't been too many roadblocks except for the occasional injury, and none of them have been life- or career-threatening. I've had a fantastic career as far as adversity."

Baze, a high-school valedictorian, is happily married to the former Tami Arterburn, a trainer's daughter. They have raised four children, ages eleven to twenty-one, in the San Francisco Bay Area. All are doing well. Baze doesn't smoke, doesn't drink, and hasn't fought since he wrestled in high school. By any objective standards, he is "normal," and as such, is the exception to the rule among his riding peers. He possesses a timely and self-skewering sense of humor and seems acutely aware of his environment, whether on horseback or in the greater race of life.

He met Tami one morning at a horse crossing at the racetrack. She had stopped to allow Russell and his mount to pass. Instead, he halted and asked if she was waiting for the light to change. Even though their parents knew each other, Russell and Tami didn't officially meet until he introduced himself shortly after that first encounter. They married in 1979. In a change of direction for both the Baze and Arterburn families, none of their children appear headed for a life at the races.

Now in his early forties, Baze realizes he is on a collision course with destiny and criticism. Both will arrive in his life for the same reason — he wins more races more often than anyone else in his profession. There is no doubt that if he remains healthy and willing, Russell Baze will, in the next five or seven or nine years, become the winningest jockey in the history of U.S. Thoroughbred racing. When he does, some will praise him for his talent and perseverance. Others will slap a Roger Maris asterisk on his mark because the lion's share of his victories have come in the Bay Area of California, a cut below the country's preeminent racetracks.

It will be no lovefest on the scale of that which greeted Laffit Pincay Jr. when he wrested the lifetime win record from Bill Shoemaker late in 1999. That coveted crown passed from John Longden to Shoemaker to Pincay in a seamless progression of riders considered the greatest of their day. Russell Baze, on the basis of capturing the great races on the grandest horses, doesn't fit the royal lineage. All he does is go out day after day and do his job — win races. He's not going to apologize for doing it better than anyone else, and he's not going to proclaim himself the next Shoemaker. Being Russell Baze has been more than good enough.

Russell was meant to be a rider from the beginning. His father, Joe Baze, won riding titles at Golden Gate Fields and Bay Meadows as well as at Longacres, Portland Meadows, and Playfair. In 1992, when Russell tallied seven winners on one card at Golden Gate to set a new record, his father was one of the riders whose mark he shattered. Joe rode for twenty-five years, including some summers up at Exhibition Park in Vancouver. Before the family could make it back to the United States in 1958, Russell was born in Canada.

He grew up out in the countryside of Washington state, where his father put his five children, four of them boys, up on Shetland and Welsh ponies when each turned four or five years old. Joe Baze later bought property in the town of Granger, in the Yakima Valley, and the family built a training ranch there. Joe broke and trained horses during the week and rode at Yakima on the weekends. During summers, the family would travel to Longacres in Seattle where Joe rode and the kids took jobs as grooms on the backside.

When Russell was ten he began working as a gofer and cleaning stalls for trainer Howard Belvoir, the patriarch of another family of prolific West Coast horsemen. For years, Russell has ridden with Vann Belvoir in the Bay Area.

Baze taking delight in a narrow decision.

Between the ranch and his racetrack work, Russell gathered considerable knowledge of the equine athlete.

"I was learning basic survival," is how Baze puts it. "Like how not to get my feet stepped on while walking hots; the places I should be so I wouldn't get kicked; how not to get bitten. For anyone who wants to work with horses, it's beneficial to start from the ground floor with basics and get to know how they think and how to take care of them." Horses were part of the youngster's recreation. Baze and his friends would trail ride and play tag on horseback.

When Russell turned twelve, his dad figured he was big enough to climb aboard some old campaigners he'd bought for the older boys to gallop and ride. By thirteen he was galloping horses and progressed from the older ones to learning how to break colts at the family farm. Older brother Jeff was the first to try his hand professionally, but he broke an ankle, and by the time it healed, he had out-grown the profession. Younger brother Dale followed Russell to the racetrack and has ridden all around the country, presently in the Midwest at tracks like Hoosier Park and Prairie Meadows.

Russell, in his early teens, continued to work summers as a groom on the racetrack, enjoying the atmosphere and the excitement. "Once I started galloping it was pretty much tunnel vision," he said. "I loved being on the race-track and really enjoyed getting on horses." Just before his sixteenth birthday Baze raced an Appaloosa at the Walla Walla County Fair and finished third.

The other activity vying for his interest was wrestling. "I thought I was pretty good," he said, "but the last match before the state tournament a kid put an illegal scissors on me. I won the match, then began coughing up blood. I decided to focus more on riding than wrestling at that point."

Thus, Baze followed a parade of relatives into the racing business. Besides his brothers, legions of cousins and uncles populate the sport. His grandmother rode horses. His uncle Basil James was leading rider in the country. A cousin, Tyler Baze, now doing well on the Southern California circuit, won the Eclipse Award for top apprentice jockey in 2000. One story has a trainer named Alton Howry attempting to engage Russell Baze's riding services. Baze's agent told Howry the rider was unavailable and, "besides, Russell doesn't even know you." Replied Howry, "I'm his uncle." Baze ended up on Howry's horse.

Once he secured his license, Russell rode weekends at Yakima, barely two years after his father had retired from riding in 1974. "A lot of people tell me he was the best rider they've ever seen," Russell says of his father. "He taught me everything about riding — how to sit in the saddle, how to throw a cross, everything. As I progressed he started teaching me the finer points like how to cock a stick and how to change sticks. Because he's right-handed and I'm left-handed, it took me awhile to learn, but as a result I'm ambidextrous."

While most jockeys learned riding from watching prominent riders in person or on film, Baze had the advantage of a live-in instructor. "My dad knew how he wanted me to do things, and he made sure I did them the right way."

Joe Baze, who trained horses until 1992 and today owns and operates a mobile-home park in Montana, said he taught his children whatever he could. "You can teach anyone the mechanics of the sport, but from there on it's natural ability that takes over. Having ridden, there are a lot of little things I told them that I learned. I told them so much they probably couldn't remember it."

Russell soaked up his father's advice, but still had to put it into practice on the racetrack. "I'd say ninety percent of riding is learned, and ten percent is God-given talent that separates the high echelon riders from the rest. I was blessed in that I had my own racetrack to learn on and was able to get such a good foundation before I went to the races and unveiled my lack of talent," Russell laughed.

Whereas his brothers and cousins all won their first or second professional race, Russell didn't break his maiden until his thirteenth start, proving the race isn't always to the swift. He piloted Oregon Warrior, trained by his dad, to the winner's circle for his first victory. When he turned seventeen, Baze's Uncle Kenny had his contract and Russell arrived to ride in the Bay Area for the first time. Two months later he returned to the Northwest with two wins and "my tail between my legs." It didn't remain there for long, as Baze soon became a top rider at Portland Meadows and rode at Yakima on the weekends until he graduated high school.

Joe Baze said Russell always had a sense of presence. "He knew what he was doing and where he was at in a race. He seemed to be born with that clock in his head where he knew how fast his horse was running compared to the rest of them. My opinion is a lot of riders may look good, but the horses don't run for them. It's something you have that can't be taught. Russell is a better rider than I was. I told him I hate to think I wasted all that time teaching him if he wasn't any better than me."

Instead of returning to Bay Meadows the following year, Russell rode at the fairs in Pomona and Fresno, and after a stint at Longacres, worked his way over to the Chicago circuit. He spent a year there, finishing second in the jockey standings at Sportsman's Park. In the fall of 1978, he was ready to return to Northern California, three years after his first experiment there. "I'm sure I was a stronger rider the second time around," Baze noted. "I had had time to hone my skills and develop confidence in myself. You get that from experience." In 1978 and '79 Baze was winning at a solid but not spectacular twelve percent. His seven stakes winners all came in the Northwest at tracks such as Longacres, Yakima, and Portland.

By 1980 his strike rate inched up to fourteen percent, and, more importantly, his six stakes winners all came at Bay Meadows, Golden Gate, and the fairs at Solano and Pleasanton. The following year, all hell broke loose. Baze won 268 races, one hundred more than he'd won in any previous year. Eighteen percent of his mounts found the winner's circle, and his stakes wins catapulted to twenty. Several factors that established Baze's dominance around San Francisco were at play.

"First, I decided to stay here year-round, and trainers are more likely to put you on their good horses when they know you're going to be around to consistently ride them and help develop the younger horses as well. Secondly, I hooked up with Ray Harris as my agent. He's a really sharp agent who was making his living as a gambler before that, so he can handicap. Those two things really gave me a boost."

Recalled Harris: "He had been staying in the Bay Area from October to March and then going back to Seattle, so I made a deal with him in 1980 that if I got him in the top five in the standings here, he'd stay for the summer. He agreed, since his wife was from this area anyway. He ended up fourth in the standings, stayed here, and he's

Baze aboard Event of the Year, one of his top mounts.

been leading rider ever since." As amazing as it seems, from 1981 through 2001, Russell Baze has won the jockey title at every Bay Meadows and Golden Gate meeting in which he's competed.

Top trainers like Jerry Hollendorfer and Greg Gilchrist were just getting started in the early eighties along with Baze, who also was helped by conditioners like Charlie Comiskey, Lavar Larson, Emmett Campbell, and Ike Orr. Hollendorfer, who dominates Northern California trainers almost as completely as does Baze its jockeys, points to Russell's personal life rather than his riding talents when asked the reason for the rider's success.

"He's disciplined, stable, a great family man, and all that allows him to concentrate on his riding. He has no bad habits," Hollendorfer said. "He's got focus every day. Whether there is a gap between him and other riders, I'm not sure, but I think there is. Perhaps it's because I've worked with him so much and have a lot of confidence in him. He gets the job done, and we've stuck together a long time."

If anything besides the right trainers and agent explains his consistency and excellence over time, it is Baze's versatility. He is impossible to pigeonhole style-wise, having never been known strictly as a speed rider or a come-from-behinder. His sense of pace is solid, and he can also shake up a horse that needs the extra incentive. "Riding as many cheap horses as I have," said Baze, "one of the things I've had to work on the most is getting out of that mentality that I have to ride 'em all hard. With good horses, I have to mentally back off sometimes because not only do they not need it, their owners get a little sensitive about you being overly aggressive."

Ray Harris says every good rider has a different style. "Some guys are aggressive, some like to come from behind, others are good thinkers. Russell is smart, and he's aggressive. He really gets after a horse and demands a lot out of them. He never gives up. If he can't win, he's gonna get second or third. He's a battler. Some guys, if they're not going to win, they wait till later. Russell doesn't have any 'wait till later' in him."

Joe Baze says his son rides harder than he did. "He finishes so hard, I don't know how he can keep going year after year like he does. When I got a little older, I just couldn't do it. I had to take off for a while every winter."

Beginning in 1988, Russell began spending some "down time" of his own at Del Mar. That summer, he captured the Coronado Stakes, the El Cajon Stakes, the Osunitas Handicap, and the Oceanside Stakes on the tougher circuit. One year later he returned to Del Mar and won three more stakes. He stayed in Southern California to score in the grade I Oak Tree Invitational Handicap aboard Hawkster at Santa Anita.

Those who question the validity of Baze's mounting win total usually challenge him to ride down south if he wants to prove his worth. He did just that from 1989 to 1991, leaving the friendly confines of the Bay Area in search of better stock and the opportunity for mounts in the classic races. It's often a matter of comparing apples with oranges, however, because new riders shipping into the Southern California jockey colony just do not get the kind of quality mounts on which they can prove themselves immediately. After conquering the Bay Area, though, Baze was ready to give it his best shot.

"I went down there with the idea of riding better horses and hopefully winning some of the bigger races. The chances to ride horses that can take you to classic wins are limited up here. But the competition for mounts there is fierce with the concentration of top riders. It's the greatest place in the world to ride. And it was a lot of fun getting on those good horses — the problem was they were letting me get on them in the morning but not in the afternoon. I really wasn't riding better horses there than I was here."

Baze did earn stakes wins aboard mounts such as Lite Light, Great Communicator, Answer Do, and Invited Guest, but his win percentage shrunk into the ten percent to twelve percent range. After being hurt in a fall, he was ready to head back north.

"I was ready to come home anyway," he said. "The handwriting was on the wall for me. I've seen guys who have been down there a long time not doing much who all of a sudden get the opportunity and turn it around. But at the time I left, I wasn't getting the chance to ride and win races. Even in the cheap races I wasn't getting the kind of horses I could win on consistently. It wasn't the kind of situation I wanted to stay in. Hey, I'm not the first guy in the world to go there and not have the success that he wanted. Anyone in the country who starts doing well gets it in their head to come to California. Looking back at the experience, I'm happy with what I did down there."

Harris said Baze actually improved as a rider when he rode down south, against the best riders in the world. "It gave him confidence that he fit with them," he said. "And when he came back up here he really dominated."

If there is a stronger word than "dominate," it applies to Baze's performance in Northern California from 1992 on. Check out these annual win percentages, beginning in

'92 — twenty-six, twenty-six, twenty-six, twenty-nine, twenty-eight, twenty-eight, twenty-seven, twenty-eight, twenty-seven, and in 2001, twenty-eight. Keep in mind that the average nationwide for all jockeys is eight percent. In only two years since 1992 has his winning percentage in stakes races dipped under twenty. And Baze was climbing aboard some nice stakes horses — the best the Bay Area had to offer, as well as Southern California shippers that come north to try and take down added-money events. Some of his multiple black-type horses included Lykatill Hil, Notorious Pleasure, Work the Crowd, Soviet Problem, Semoran, Traces of Gold, Event of the Year, Lexicon, and Dixie Dot Com. He's won stakes aboard standouts like Queens Court Queen, Cavonnier, Pike Place Dancer, and Worldly Ways.

Behind the soft-spoken exterior, Baze pushed himself hard to achieve. Some have noted he is unapproachable after losing, but Baze downplays that perception. "I don't think I'm any different from the other guys — there's nobody out there who likes losing, as far as I can tell. In general I take defeat pretty well because it's inevitable — you're not going to win every race. I'm realistic about it, but I don't like losing, especially when I know I've made a mistake that's cost me a chance to win a race. That's when I'm upset. My brothers and I were competitive; the whole family was competitive. When my cousins came over, we'd always be wrestling or seeing who could jump highest over a broom handle. So that's innate."

Unquestioned is Baze's work ethic, which is unusual for a rider in his position. In a normal week, he's out at the track six mornings working horses. "I like to know how the horses are doing training up to a race," he said. "I enjoy

63

getting up and doing something in the morning, or else I'd be sitting around the house probably eating too much. And the trainers like to see you out there. It lets them know you're still interested."

Harris says Baze doesn't have to be at the track that many mornings a week. "Guys in his position might have cut down a long time ago, but he keeps working and he deserves what he gets."

Because Baze wins so much, one wonders if his fellow riders might resent his success. Baze understands that dynamic, yet says he has a good relationship with other jockeys. "You can't blame them for being disgruntled when one guy's winning the lion's share of the races," he said. "I don't lord it over them or rub it in. I don't have any real enemies out there."

Baze was asked how he would answer someone who grouses that he gets all the good mounts. "First, I'd have to agree with them," he said. "Nobody is gonna win a bunch of races unless you get the stock to ride. That's a fact of life. But it's not like the same opportunity isn't available to any-one out there. You just have to show the talent and the will to do it, and there's no saying that somebody else can't have the same kind of success."

The one area where Baze hasn't enjoyed success is in the prestigious classic races. His only Breeders' Cup mount was a twelfth aboard Lite Light in the 1990 Juvenile Fillies, and his lone Kentucky Derby mount was Semoran, who finished fourteenth in the 1996 running. His best chance to contend for the roses to date was 1998, when he partnered with Event of the Year to capture the El Camino Real Derby at Bay Meadows and followed up three weeks later with a devastating score in the Jim Beam Stakes at

Turfway Park. Event of the Year, a son of Seattle Slew trained by Hollendorfer, looked to be a major contender, if not the favorite, for the Derby, but suffered a slab fracture of the knee and remained on the sidelines.

"A lot of people ask if I was nervous riding in the 1996 Derby, but I had made up my mind to take in the whole atmosphere, and it was so exciting and interesting being there I wasn't nervous at all," Baze said. "The crowd is huge. It was so cool seeing that many people in one place, people hanging over the fences by the jocks' room. It wasn't emotional because it was so loud I couldn't hear 'My Old Kentucky Home.' As far as the race itself, it was just another race except there were a bunch more horses out there.

"Like everybody else, I'd like to win the Derby and some Breeders' Cup races, but I don't set my sights on them. I don't really set a lot of goals other than to go out and win every race I ride. People ask me if I have a goal to win four hundred every year. I don't. I try and win as many as I can every year, every day, and it will all work itself out."

Baze realizes that unless an outstanding horse starts out in Northern California, the chance of his getting the mount in classic races is small. Good horses already have regular riders when they make it into stakes company, and even when trainers play musical chairs with riders, they're unlikely to reach out to another circuit to come up with a rider. Even when Baze wins stakes aboard shippers to Northern California, he rarely retains the mount when the horse returns home. "I don't worry about that a whole lot," he said. "I take what is offered me and am happy for it. I wouldn't rule out somebody coming and putting me on a top horse, but I'm not gonna hold my breath."

All he does is win his four hundred races a year, a feat he accomplished seven consecutive years until an injury in the fall of 1999 allowed him to win "just" 373. No other rider has won four hundred races more than three times in a career. In 1996 the National Turf Writers Association began presenting the Isaac Murphy Award to the rider with the highest annual winning percentage. After seven years, Baze is still the only jockey to have won it.

Laffit Pincay, as of this writing, is some 1,500 wins beyond Baze, and the math says that if both continue at their current pace (not even taking into account the older Pincay is likely to retire first), Baze will eventually outdistance him. Racing purists will point out that while Pincay has enjoyed a legendary career, Baze has won exactly three grade I races: the 1984 Oak Tree Invitational with Both Ends Burning, the 1989 edition of the same race aboard Hawkster, and the 1991 Santa Monica Handicap with Devil's Orchid.

"I don't even dignify that with an answer," Baze said. "Winning a horse race is winning a horse race, whether you're doing it at Santa Anita or Boise, Idaho. It's just as hard to win horse races anywhere you go. You can't take anything away from the fact that Laffit has done it on the toughest circuit in the world. He's done it on a tougher circuit than I have, that's true. He's down there and I'm here. That criticism doesn't bother me. I'm not thinking about leaving here. I'm very happy right where I'm at."

Where Baze is at is in racing's Hall of Fame, inducted in 1999, a vote that he says surprised him. "I guess if I thought about it I'd think, 'Yeah, I've won a lot of races and probably do deserve to be in there,' but I don't usually think of myself along those terms. It's quite an honor. And so was getting the Special Eclipse Award I received for being the only jockey to win four hundred or more races four consecutive years. It's nice that I haven't gone completely unrecognized."

When asked to name his best mounts, Baze mentions horses like Hawkster, Simply Majestic, Event of the Year, and Soviet Problem. But he has a special place in his heart for the less talented ones that tried hardest, horses like Sekondi. "He was my favorite for a long time because he'd come from the clouds and give you a big kick for a quarter mile. He had a lot of problems that would have kept a lesser horse from running at all, yet he'd always go out there and give you that run. There have been a lot of horses like that through the years — cheap horses that had every reason not to run, who still went out there and gave you their best every time."

Though he may ride cheap horses, there is nothing inherent in that that gives cause to disparage his skills as a jockey or the drive that pushes him onward, quite possibly to the very top of his profession. Every time he goes out on the track, Russell Baze gives you his best. And that's been plenty good enough.

4

JORGE CHAVEZ

Rags to Roses

It's Belmont Stakes week, 2001, and Jorge Chavez, four weeks removed from his greatest victory, walks toward Belmont Park's jockeys' room after winning a turf race. A woman leans over the railing, calls his name, and shares a picture of Chavez visiting her gravely ill daughter in the hospital. The little girl had since passed away. "I wanted to tell you how much it meant to us, you coming to see her," the woman told Chavez. He had stopped now in front of her, not as a celebrity, but as a caring individual. She handed him a keepsake from the girl, and he kissed it and made the sign of the cross while looking through the grandstand to the heavens. As Chavez moved off down the tunnel, she called after him, "Georgie, an angel rides on your shoulder."

If an angel had been watching Jorge Chavez for his forty-plus years, it would have witnessed one bumpy journey endured by the Peruvian jockey, who feels for children so much because of the shattered family, poverty, and street life of his own youth. Where many a person has been broken by a hardscrabble childhood, Chavez said, "It made me keep going, motivated me to a better life and to success."

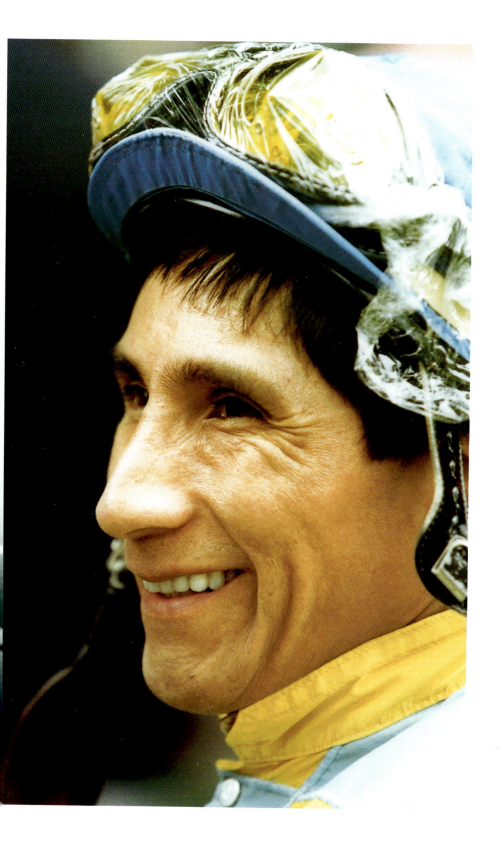

Chavez is the best kind of hero for his adopted homeland, New York. Jerry Bailey dominates the jockey colony,
but his coolness runs counter to the culture of the city. The
diminutive Chavez, standing well on the shy side of five
feet, burns hot. You can see it in his South American
Indian features, and you can hear it from the railbirds and
paddock-liners who affectionately call his name at every
chance. Well, not his real name. After all, he's in New York
now. "Bring him home, Georgie."

Although he's short even by jockey standards and an
instant underdog by any measure, he's a good guy, honest
and hard working to a fault. The biggest knock against
him was that he worked too hard encouraging his mounts
with the stick during races, earning him the nickname
"Chop Chop." His former agent, Richard DePass, says the
nickname is unfair and explained that Jorge is just smaller than the other guys, so he needs to move his body more
when he goes to the whip. Additionally, finishing second
rather than third or fourth means something in dollars
when you're hungry. Literally hungry, as Chavez was when
he first came to America. That's when you really try hard.

In case anyone missed Chavez' coming-out party in 1999
when he won the Eclipse Award as the nation's outstanding
jockey, Chavez cut the cake again in 2001 with his stirring
Kentucky Derby victory aboard Monarchos. It was a classic
Derby performance, his horse weaving out and in from far
back, holes opening seemingly on cue, leading to a huge
sweep past the field in dominating fashion. "The first thing
I thought was 'I won the Derby,' " he said. "Then I started
wondering if it was a dream, if it's too good to be true."

Chavez can be forgiven his temporary skepticism.
There was precious little of any good in his early years.

70

Born in 1961, he was sent at an impossibly early age — "three or five" — to live at his grandfather's farm, where he used to ride donkeys and horses to help work the fields. His parents' lives together had already torn apart. Chavez thinks he could have a dozen brothers and sisters. There are only three that he knows to visit today.

When he was seven, Jorge went to live with his father in Lima. He was shuttled between his mother's and father's new families, fitting in nowhere, usually hungry. "Growing up, I was never happy," Chavez told Scott Davis in an article in *The Blood-Horse* in 2000. "I was never part of a real family. Even when I left, there was no love. Nobody ever asked if I had enough to eat or clothes to wear."

That was at age ten. It seems unbelievable that the man Chavez is today — kind, friendly, considerate — could possibly have emerged from the streets of Lima so unscathed by the meanness of his reality. Perhaps the legend has grown through the years and exaggerates the truth. "No, it is true; I was living in the streets and out of cars," Chavez said matter-of-factly. "But if you're going to survive somehow you have to get through it. I'm not the only one from my country who has to live that way. If you go to my country, you'll see a lot of children like that today. Maybe worse than what I went through.

"I see the children sometimes who have disease...that girl in the picture, that makes me feel bad because you don't want to see children die. They don't know anything about life. That's sad. You don't ever want to see anything happen to children."

By his own count, Chavez worked "hundreds of different jobs" as he grew up. He might not have made candlesticks, but he did work as a butcher, a baker, an appliance repairman, construction worker, and bus driver. He returned to his mother's home one last time, at age fifteen. But after a sister committed suicide, he left for good. At nineteen he went to the racetrack one day and fell in love with the horses. He decided to try to get work there, but since he didn't know anybody, the guards wouldn't let him in.

Finally he began working at the bottom, cleaning stalls, and then progressed to grooming. Chavez realized his size was ideal for being a jockey, and gradually he was introduced to some trainers and began learning to gallop horses, working them from the gate. At age twenty-two he took his test from the gate for the stewards and got a riding license. He made up for his late start by watching taped races from the United States.

Chavez gave Monarchos a brilliant ride in the 2001 Kentucky Derby.

"I used to watch Pincay and Shoemaker on the tapes; that's how I started, just watching them," said Chavez. "More than anything else I tried to just go in stride with the horse without moving around and causing him to lose stride. It's not easy — you have to do it step by step. Every horse is different. Some move quickly, some have longer or shorter strides, some are lazy, some have speed. There's a lot of things to learn. It takes time, and you have to be very patient to learn. Even today I'm still learning. Nobody can say 'I know everything about life or I know everything about horses.' It's not true. Every year you never stop learning, no matter how old you get to be."

Chavez hooked up with trainer Juan Suarez, Peru's longtime leading conditioner, and became the barn's regular rider. His first win came July 15, 1982, when he rode Marst to victory. By 1986 Chavez was the leading rider at Hipodromo Monterico in Peru, a feat he repeated in 1987. A year later he traveled to Florida on vacation. A friend suggested he try riding there. It must have gone well because he stayed. He became the leading rider at Calder and the Tropical-at-Calder meeting that same year. In 1989 he garnered ninety-three wins at the seventy-one-day Hialeah meeting, setting a record. He topped that off by capturing the riding title at Gulfstream Park that year.

Chavez said that riding in Florida was no different than riding in Peru, with one exception. "The big difference was the money involved. I rode two winners my second day there and got a check for five thousand dollars. I couldn't believe it." Chavez was here to stay, but not without problems.

Apparently, some of the other riders in the Florida jockey colony were not overcome by the feel-good story of the

Peruvian who excelled in his new home. "I was winning races, and there were some jealousies with the other riders," said Chavez. "They began riding me a little rough, and I just gave it back to them. Plus, I didn't speak English at that time so I couldn't explain to the stewards what I was doing or what they were doing to me. So I got in trouble."

Chavez became well acquainted with the stewards who handed him more than his fair share of suspensions. He sat out twenty-five days at his first meeting, Tropical-at-Calder, and somehow managed to double that during the regular Calder meet. Hialeah was relatively uneventful, as Chavez was given ten days during that engagement. Perhaps part of the improvement was due to his efforts to learn the language. Chavez began speaking English with friends as much as possible and carried around a Spanish-English dictionary. The book helped him explain himself to stewards as well.

As the eighties melted away, Chavez moved his tack north from Florida to New York. His consistency throughout the nineties was amazing — the win totals beginning in 1990 read 244, 214, 168, 244, 228, 249, 246, 259, 253, then a whopping 320 in his breakout year of 1999. But until 1999, despite constantly ranking at or near the top of the circuit's leading riders, Chavez could not shake his reputation of being overly aggressive. That is why so much is made of his riding style. Is it that he must reach farther back with the whip because of his short stature and gives the impression of hitting the mount harder than he actually is, or is he over-aggressive?

"I'm aggressive, but maybe not enough for some people," Chavez said. "In the beginning I was just trying to win the most I can with anything I can. It's like when you stay in one place doing nothing, then you go outside and you're so desperate to eat. When I saw my first check I was hungry to eat and trying to survive. Every ride was important, every second and third. And to me it still is, although not for survival anymore."

Trainer and Chavez patron John Ward Jr. said the overly aggressive reputation didn't fit the jockey. "He wouldn't do anything in the world to abuse a horse," said Ward. "He was self-taught as a race rider in Peru. You can see the evolution in the last five or six years from someone who rode as hard as he could to someone who's gone to finesse. He's maturing as a race rider now."

Chavez plugged away in the early nineties, putting up strong numbers but rarely getting top stock to sit aboard. Through 1998 he won seven Aqueduct riding titles and another three at Belmont. In the middle of the decade, his roster of mounts became sprinkled with recognizable names. Chavez partnered with Will's Way to take the 1996 Travers. He won the Met Mile on You and I in 1995, and two years later repeated with Langfuhr. In 1996 he and Diplomatic Jet took down the Early Times Manhattan, the Turf Classic Invitational, and the Man o' War.

Unlike many other riders who study their opponents, take into account what rider is on which horse, and try to anticipate what each will do at certain junctures in the race, Chavez only cares about riding his horse. "I don't think about anyone else out there," he noted. "I don't care what the other guy is doing in a race. I just want to do my job. I know how I can win and I do my thing. I don't ride the other horses. I ride my own horse."

Chavez' purse earnings bolted from the six-million-dollar range in 1993 and 1994 to nine million dollars

annually from 1996 to 1998. Along came the speedy
Affirmed Success, who won the 1998 Vosburgh with
Chavez, the Forego Handicap the same year, and the Cigar
Mile in 1999. Trainer James Bond, who put Chavez aboard
Diplomatic Jet and Will's Way, also gave him a leg up on

*Chavez savored his victory aboard Beautiful Pleasure in
the 1999 Breeders' Cup Distaff.*

his top handicap runner, Behrens, throughout 1999, when the colt won the Gulfstream Park Handicap, the Oaklawn Handicap, and the Suburban. "Chavez has the greatest work ethic in the world," Bond told *The Blood-Horse*, "a strong will to win, and a continually positive attitude."

Although Chavez was the leading rider in New York for five consecutive years, from 1994 to 1998, he had yet to break through consistently into the top echelon of mounts. He decided that after ten years away, he would return to Florida in 1999 for the winter meeting at Gulfstream. "I won the title down there and picked up good mounts, and that made the difference," said Chavez. "I was riding the same, but I was on better horses, and all of a sudden people start looking at me in a different way."

Chavez picked up the business on Artax, a horse that had shown talent early on the West Coast but faltered as the races got longer and the competition stiffer. Shifted to the East Coast, Paraneck Stables and trainer Louis Albertrani decided to turn Artax back in distance. Sprinting, with Chavez on his back, the son of Marquetry turned into a monster, winning the Carter Handicap and the Vosburgh.

"Artax always had a problem breaking a step slow from the gate," said Albertrani. "But he accelerated out of there with George. Fit him perfectly. George is a wonderful rider, and the classiest person you'd ever want to be around. He's one of those guys who's always in a good mood. Nothing gets him down race after race. And he'll ride a cheap horse as hard as he'll ride a good one. He's hard working and aggressive, and that's part of why we put him on Artax. We were looking for someone to get into the horse a little more."

Chavez also steered Artax clear of a nut who jumped onto the Pimlico racing surface and tried to hit the horse on Preakness Day 1999. The jockey's quick thinking prevented a disaster.

At the same time Chavez captured the attention of trainers John and Donna Ward, who condition their horses a furlong away from Keeneland in Lexington, Kentucky, as did John's father, uncle, and grandfather. The Wards rode Chavez on Pyramid Peak at Saratoga in 1998, and they came back winners, marking the beginning of a beautiful friendship.

"We watched him closely and realized he was an aggressive rider, but as far as the horse was concerned, he protected the horse very well," John Ward said. "So we went ahead and used him and found he was a rider who will give you his all on every horse. That's his trademark. What amazed me is he could be running last on a horse, and he'll still be riding, trying to teach the horse something so that next time he rode back he could have a better performance."

Donna Ward also selected Chavez to ride the Maudlin filly Beautiful Pleasure, a powerhouse just hitting her peak in 1999. Together they took the Beldame and the Personal Ensign. As the autumn of 1999 arrived and the Breeders' Cup unfolded at Gulfstream Park, Chavez had live mounts all over the card with Quiet Resolve, Val's Prince, Behrens, Artax, and Beautiful Pleasure. He was also carrying a zero-for-nineteen Breeders' Cup record into the day.

"I wasn't feeling any pressure," remembered Chavez, "because I never had the chance to ride good enough horses. I know I'm a good jockey, and I know what I can do. Finally, I got the opportunity, and it was a different game. I wasn't trying to prove anything to anybody, but it feels great to win because sometimes you have good horses and still don't make it. So it was a beautiful thing."

Chavez went after it right from the start of the Distaff. He let Beautiful Pleasure roll after Heritage of Gold through punishing fractions, had the lead before four furlongs were completed, and held off Banshee Breeze late for his first Breeders' Cup win. Three races later he put the exclamation mark on the day when he brought Artax to the front around the turn and kept him going ahead of Kona Gold and Big Jag to win the Sprint. On November 6, 1999, Jorge Chavez hit the map that the racing world uses to chart success. It was the day "Chop Chop" ceased to be an indictment and became just an endearing nickname.

When the calendar turned to 2000 and the stats from 1999 were tallied, Chavez finished with a remarkable 320 wins good for $17,217,417, nearly double his best year up till then. He not only led New York in wins for the sixth straight year, not only led all New York riders in purse money earned, but finally won an Eclipse Award as the nation's outstanding jockey as well. Business picked up, and Chavez has been riding better horses ever since that Breeders' Cup Day.

One of those, Monarchos, a gray son of Maria's Mon trained by John Ward, was a late bloomer on the three-year-old scene of 2001. He was also a late runner. "Georgie's best horses traditionally had a natural amount of speed," said Ward. "He's now acquired a new style recently where he's gotten very good timing coming from off the pace. On Monarchos you saw the new Georgie."

When Monarchos made a devastating move around the far turn to bury the Florida Derby field in March, he stamped himself as a Kentucky Derby contender. A second-place effort in the Wood Memorial took some of the sheen off Monarchos — until the first Saturday in May.

Under hot, sunny conditions in the Kentucky Derby, Monarchos and Chavez steamed from the back of the field, flew past favorite Point Given, and were much the best down the length of the Churchill Downs stretch.

"When I was an apprentice in Peru, I knew the Kentucky Derby was one of the prestigious races, one of the greatest races you can win," Chavez said. "There are so many feelings right after, cold and hot, and mentally you think so many things, your happiness, and you don't know where you are. It's an unbelievable, amazing feeling. Your mind goes from one thing to another to another. You're all over the place."

Afterward, Ward and Monarchos' owners, Debby and John Oxley, stressed the teamwork concept that it took to win the Derby, including Chavez as a special part of the package. "He comes by the barn and is very in tune with our horses," said John Ward. "And we're very in tune with him and his family. Georgie's very humorous when you get to know him and you can finally understand what he's saying." Facing the media, Chavez, who now speaks serviceable, if not perfect, English, could barely find the words. He seemed to be floating several feet above the platform.

"My life hasn't changed," Chavez said a month after winning the Derby. "I've always been friendly with a lot of people, and I'm still the same. Sometimes now when I go somewhere people will come up to me and say my face looks familiar, or 'hey, I know you, you won the Kentucky Derby.' They ask me to sign, and it's good."

Chavez now has a happy family life of his own. He and his second wife, Margarita, had twin daughters in 1998. The couple is also raising Margarita's two children from a previous marriage. Chavez said that his difficult childhood hasn't affected his own family life.

"I'm a good father and a good husband, and my wife and I talk like friends. I can tell her everything." He did, however, lose a custody battle with his first wife over Jorge Jr., born in 1988. They have moved from Peru to New York, but Chavez doesn't see his son nearly as much as he'd like, and that causes him sadness because of his sensitivity to growing up without proper attention. "My ex-wife tells me he doesn't want to see me, but I don't think that's true. I try to do things for him, but sometimes they don't work out. I don't want him to go through what I went through. I'll wait and hope that one day he'll grow up and see what kind of father he has."

Chavez the jockey has made an indelible mark on his native Peru. Lima now has a riding school, due in part to Chavez' popularity, and more Peruvians are coming to America to try and follow in his footsteps. Chavez donated an Exercizer to the riding school so that jockeys could practice their craft. He travels back to his homeland once or twice a year, preferring not to tell anybody so that he can keep a low profile. "If people know, then the newspapers come over and people are everywhere and you can't even walk," he said. "You don't want that for five or seven days. You want to be able to do what you want to do. I go to see one brother and two sisters and some friends.

"I see the children in the street selling candies and drinks and I give them money — five or ten dollars makes their day, and the children smile and it's the most beautiful thing."

Oh Happy Day

Bruce Springsteen's lyric "It's so hard to be a saint in the city" could have been written for Pat Day. The words fit the Hall of Fame jockey in both of his stark incarnations — the hell-raising, hot-tempered, substance-abusing, yet successful young jockey; and later the deeply religious, Bible-quoting, patient rider who has risen to the top of his profession.

Day's story is written in his face, the deep lines of experience speaking volumes.

The irony that he has devoted his life to Christian values while making his living off the ungodly act of gambling is not lost on Day. He said he searched his soul and prayed to make sure his involvement in horse racing did not affront his religion. It's so hard to be a saint in the city.

Day's origins are a long way off from the city. He grew up on a small ranch in Eagle, Colorado, a son of an auto body and fender repairman who had been raised on a South Dakota ranch. There were some chickens and horses, a milk cow, a brother, and two sisters. Day's love of horses came from helping his father break and train horses from neighboring ranches.

"My father wouldn't let us use a saddle when we started out," remembered Day. "He said, 'I want you to learn to ride the horse, not the saddle.' And so we had to ride bare-back for the longest time before he purchased a saddle for us. And I think that has helped me tremendously in my riding."

Although he had a few pangs about not living in town with the other kids, Day is thankful for the time in the country. While in high school, he flitted from job to job — working at a dude ranch, as a plumber's helper, as a carpenter's helper, stacking sheet rock, and operating a chairlift at a Vail ski resort. After graduating, he managed a gas station for a year, all the while keeping alive a dream.

"I wanted to be a professional bull rider," Day said. "I loved the mystique and the nomadic lifestyle of a cowboy, chasing from town to town, wild and free."

And so on the weekends Day rode the bulls at rodeos, learning the valuable lesson of how to fall. He credits the rodeo circuit with teaching him how to avoid injury, one of the constant challenges of his riding career. "I've taken a number of tumbles, but I've been able to go with the flow, to tuck and roll and relax and not tense up when that kind of situation evolves, and I'm certain that's helped me to walk away from a number of spills."

At rodeos his short stature led many people to ask whether Pat had ever been a jockey, and suggest he become one. Although Day and his siblings had grown up riding ponies up and down the road, this was the first he'd heard of Thoroughbred racing.

At nineteen, and with the rodeo season over, Day decided to check out the jockey business. A connection got him a job out in California at the Riverside

Thoroughbred Farm of famous trainer Farrell Jones. The plan was to learn the racing business at the farm, from the ground up, for two years, then go to the racetrack under contract for somebody and gallop, exercise, and work horses for another year.

After a month at the farm, working from daylight to dark seven days a week for minimal pay, Day yearned to go back to riding bulls and bareback horses. "Knowing nothing about the racetrack, I really didn't know what I was trying to become, so I didn't have this overwhelming desire to

An early victory at Prescott Downs in Arizona.

become a jockey," Day said. "I didn't have a clue, and I was looking at three years before I was going to participate in the competition. My competitive juices started to flow, and I didn't want to wait that long."

After failing to land a rodeo job in Las Vegas, Day hooked up with trainer Steve Talbot and began galloping horses for him. Talbot, who also served as the clerk of scales for the fair circuit in Arizona, taught Day how to ride Thoroughbreds. Soon Day found himself in Arizona riding for trainer Karl Pew, who had also been a rodeo guy, a calf-roper, so the two had common ground. "I started working all the time around the barn, and I couldn't get enough of it," said Day. "Karl held my contract and allowed me to ride some of his lesser horses, and I loved it right off the bat. I rode a couple of weekends before I broke my maiden on a horse called Forblunged for a six-hundred-dollar pot. I got thirty-six dollars and thought I'd died and gone to heaven. I didn't think it got any better than that."

Less than a year later Day was the leading rider at Turf Paradise in Phoenix despite admitting that he really didn't know what he was doing. "If you sat down and talked to me after a race, I didn't have a clue what I'd just done. It's like somebody that picks up a basketball and it's nothing but net, or picks up a golf club and whack, right down the fairway. I believe I was a natural to a large degree, a diamond in the rough.

"I've heard people say that a good rider is born and not made, and I think that's true to a certain extent. There is an intuitiveness, a sense and a feel that the top riders have. There's always a learning curve, but I believe I inherited horsemanship skills and abilities. It's where God intended me to be because I've been blessed with ability and talent and a gift of knowing intuitively when and how to move."

The great riders and trainers can communicate with their horses. The legendary jockey Eddie Arcaro would talk about the difference between himself and Bill Shoemaker, convinced that he was a better, smarter, and stronger rider than his rival. The difference, Arcaro said, was that horses seemed to want to run for Shoemaker, whereas he had to make them run. Day is cognizant of his mount the moment he walks into the paddock. He begins watching the horse, looking at his eyes and his body movements. The physical contact comes when he is hoisted aboard.

"I find that I'm able to get a horse to relax and settle in stride and conserve his energy, and that they're responsive in giving me their best with minimal encouragement on my part. That's been true throughout my career, and I believe that's my greatest attribute as a rider. The majority of all that is God-given."

In 1976, at age twenty-two, Day's name became more prominent as he began winning stakes throughout the Midwest and East. He took down the Jockey Club Gold Cup and Lawrence Realization at Belmont aboard Great Contractor, and also won the Test at Saratoga and the Sheepshead Bay at Aqueduct that year. As the decade turned, Day's win percentage climbed to the high teens, and he became a regular stakes winner at Arlington Park, Churchill Downs, and Keeneland. In 1982 Day's win percentage hit twenty-one percent and in 1983 soared to a whopping twenty-six percent.

That year Day rode stakes winners in every part of the country: he scored in the Razorback and Oaklawn Park handicaps; the Bewitch at Keeneland; the Arlington Classic and the Stars and Stripes; the Inglewood at Hollywood Park; the Travers at Saratoga; the Secretariat back at Arlington; the Spinster at Keeneland. He won forty-three stakes races in all, one out of every three in which he rode. And yet there was trouble in paradise.

"My ego got way out of line," said Day, "and I had a tendency to rear back and slap myself on the back and commend myself on doing such a fine job. In reality, I had a horrible attitude and disposition, and a terrible temper. When you're suddenly thrust into the limelight, making quick money, you have all the makings of disaster. You're made to feel important, invincible. You can get away with anything. 'I'm King Kong here.' And the negative habits latch right into you. Initially it's just to have fun — you drink and party and carry on all night — working in the daytime and rockin' and rollin' all night. You're nineteen, twenty-five, and you consider yourself indestructible. I didn't know how to handle it."

Looking now at the seemingly unflappable, more mature Pat Day, it is hard to imagine him the young hellion, starting bar brawls and getting arrested on drunk-and-disorderly charges. But that was the reality. He was convicted of marijuana possession, a misdemeanor. Cocaine binges came and went and came again. "I didn't do anything halfway," he acknowledges. "It was full bore ahead or not at all. The addictive behavior, when I jumped into that it was with both feet. I'm grateful that in my drunken and drug-induced stupors, the only one I ever hurt was myself, because it could have easily been worse. When you're out of control, you're out of control."

He married the daughter of a rider, but the relationship

went sour after the couple moved to New York. Although Day was riding well, the marriage capsized and fell apart, and soon Pat found himself alone in the big city, lonely, estranged, and with a broken heart. "That all made me use more and pay attention less," he said. "And then my riding suffered. From the outside it still seemed I was doing fairly well, but I was self-destructing, and on a one-way street to hell. I was slowly dying on the vine."

Indeed, Day appeared to be doing well. On the final day of 1982, he rushed to Delta Downs in Louisiana and won two races to defeat Angel Cordero Jr. for the year's most wins. Day saw it as testimony to his innate talent, that even with a loss of focus, his abilities still shone brightly once the gates opened.

A year after winning that riding title, Day flew into Miami in January of 1984 to ride a horse for trainer Shug McGaughey at Hialeah. In his hotel room the night before the race, Day fell into a deep sleep. He awoke a short time later with the sensation that he was not alone. Turning on the TV, he saw an evangelist having an altar call. "I knew then that Jesus was there with me," Day said, "and I had the choice of committing my life to Him. The only thing I brought to the table was a willingness to accept him into my life." Day said he fell to the floor crying, feeling finally that he had found what he was searching for. He won the race the following day. And he lost his craving for alcohol and drugs.

"I've never been one to follow stats," Day said, "but from that day on the success I've enjoyed and my achievements have gone straight up. I got back on track and realized I'd been blessed with a great deal of talent and ability, and I needed to do the very best with it that I could. Now

I have an overwhelming desire to do that which I know to be right in the eyes of God. I want to do my best when I'm riding. I want to do my best when I'm mingling with people. I am a representative of Him, and allow Him to work in and through me to accomplish things."

The racetrack is no church sanctuary. It can be a rough and tumble place of low tolerance toward many things, and certainly Day's high visibility and frequent testimony to God are not universally appreciated. When a microphone is placed in front of him, eyes begin to roll and heads shake. Racing and religion are not the easiest of mixtures, and some believe enough preaching has been done. "I hear that periodically, not a lot," Day said. "Does it bother me? No. In Jesus' words, 'if you're ashamed of me before man, I'll be ashamed of you before my Father who art in heaven.' Certainly I'm not hanging on the cross, but I recall the words of Jesus as the crowd was mocking Him. 'Father, forgive them, for they know not what they do.' So when I feel that happening that is my response. The Bible teaches us to pray for those who would spitefully abuse or persecute you, and so I do."

To his credit, Day is unfailingly polite and while religious, steers clear of displaying a 'holier than thou' attitude. Shortly after winning his eight thousandth race, Day was given a memento of that moment — a picture of himself in the winner's circle. He was carrying the large package back to the jockeys' room at Churchill Downs, but stopped and put it down each time he was asked for an autograph. He signed nine trading cards for one fan and then was approached by another autograph-seeker who saw Day struggling to carry the picture. "I'll try and catch you later," the fan said. Day immediately put down the photo. "You better catch me now," he replied, and happily signed his autograph.

The esteem in which he is held by the people of the Midwest, particularly Kentucky, is unmatched. No matter what type of stock he rides, Day is bet down below what the horse would go off at with any other rider on its back.

And Day's affection for Kentucky is mutual, although it was an accident that prompted him to make his base there. In the late seventies, Day was riding New Orleans in the winter and Chicago for much of the other three seasons. In 1979 at Sportsman's Park, he took a bad spill, which Day admitted "kinda put a fear in me."

Recently married to his second wife, Sheila, Day settled in Kentucky in the spring of 1980 rather than return to Chicago. "Back then they ran an extended summer meet at Churchill, and we were having a good amount of success," he recalled. "There were short fields and I'd have my pick of who to ride in each race. For years when I came to Kentucky I guess you could say I was a big fish in a little pond. The quality of the riders and the horses in the Midwest has gotten significantly better over the years as the purse structures have grown at Churchill and Keeneland. My agents have done a tremendous job — when I first started, I didn't have much say in picking and choosing horses. But today I'm in a very enviable position of being able to do that."

Fred Aime, who had worked for Eddie Delahoussaye, Jerry Bailey, and Randy Romero, hooked up with Day in 1985 and remained his agent until retiring ten years later. "Pat was a quality rider who got a lot of run out of horses, and he was getting popular at that time," Aime said. "He was a rising star, and with my connections and his ability

I thought we could do great things together. You know, all riders cost the same, so people look for the hottest jockey available, and with Pat we were able to pick and choose instead of hustling for mounts.

"He's a naturally likable person, a lot of class, and he's a sit-still rider; he doesn't get in the horse's way. Personally, he's a very pleasant man to work for. He didn't tell me what horses to put him on, and I didn't tell him how to ride."

Day deflects most credit to his Maker and his mounts. "The primary ingredient is the horse, and I've been blessed with the opportunity to ride good horses. And you don't have to ride a fast horse, you just have to ride one that's faster than the rest in that race. I look at the past performances and see how I think the race will shape up. I study my horse at length if I haven't ridden him, and if I have, I keep a little book where I make notes of what I've learned and rerun their previous races in my head.

"I process all this information and then kind of put it in neutral once the doors open, because you have to see how the horse comes away from there. If the race starts to unfold in the way I anticipated, then I'll go with Plan A. Plan B is to ad lib, and that's probably my second-greatest asset — intuitiveness and ability to play it off the break."

Day has earned a couple of nicknames for his riding prowess. One is "PayDay" for the frequency of his victories, and another is "Patient Pat" for his reputation of waiting until the last possible moment before urging his mount down the stretch. Like Delahoussaye, another rider perceived as a come-from-behind specialist, Day bristles a bit at being stereotyped as a one-trick pony. "Riding style is your reaction in any given race," he said. "I think I'm proficient on the front end getting horses to relax, and I'm proficient with horses coming from off the pace. I can be patient or aggressive. With Tank's Prospect in the Preakness in 1985, I got as aggressive as anybody could have in order to get the job done.

"But I'll let a horse cook along there and just get up in the last coupla jumps, or I'll be on the lead and let others go past and then come back and get a horse on the wire. I can't tell you going in that I'll be doing that. It depends on how the horses run and how mine's feeling. If someone's making a big move at the quarter pole and my horse is offering some resistance but just wants to stay there, well, that's fine, because they pay off at the

Lil E. Tee brought Day his elusive Derby victory in 1992.

wire, not at the eighth pole or the sixteenth pole. And I have a keen sense of how much horse I have left, and I'm able to squeeze him and get that last lunge and be there in front."

Trainer Elliott Walden gives Day first call on ninety percent of his starters. Their association goes back to 1985, when Day delivered Walden his first winner at Keeneland. "I had Sibling, who ran opening day and he finished tenth, beaten nine and a half lengths going six furlongs," recalled the trainer. "I was so mad at the horse for not doing any running, I entered him right back for a race four days later. One of the reasons was that I got Pat Day for that next race. Well, Pat coaxed him to the lead and nursed him around there and he won by five."

Trainer D. Wayne Lukas has had a tremendous amount of success after giving Day a leg up on his horses. Together they have won Breeders' Cup races with Cat Thief and Flanders, and the Belmont Stakes with Commendable. "When I first started using him, I didn't think Pat rode sprinters as well," said Lukas, "and I was wrong about that. We train our horses to be aggressive, with speed, and Pat has made that adjustment on our horses remarkably well.

"But his real strength is his quiet confidence," Lukas maintains. "He's at peace with himself and not fighting any outside demons. When he rides for you, you feel he's going to be in tune and focused, and you just feel good about the situation. Today so many riders seem almost turbulent in their personalities and dispositions. Pat's quiet peace is very refreshing. In a lot of ways he's the exception. Though most of the better riders have that makeup, he personifies it."

Day has been involved in many great racing moments, including his magnificent win in the inaugural Breeders' Cup Classic at Hollywood Park in 1984. He was aboard the second-longest shot in the field, 31-1 Wild Again, whose owners had to pay $360,000 to supplement him into the race, meaning they had more confidence in their horse than did the betting public. Wild Again had a tendency to drift out because he had a foot that turned out, Day said, and blacksmith Jack Reynolds got him as good as he could.

"All things being equal, he was up against it," Day admitted. "Wild Again grabbed the bit and ran off, right past Slew o' Gold's rabbit into the first turn. When we got to the head of the stretch, Slew o' Gold ran up on our outside and I figured, 'Well, that's it.' In past races, when the real running started, Wild Again just hung it up. But now he wouldn't let Slew o' Gold by. Now we're brushing and I'm dragging him in and dragging him in trying to keep him running, and here comes Gate Dancer too. It was a great race. A great race. I can close my eyes today and hear Wild Again grunting: 'Uuuuh. Uuuuh. Uuuuh.' He was fighting for it. I'd never been on a horse that showed that kind of intestinal fortitude."

Day was also in the middle of the great 1989 rivalry between Sunday Silence and Easy Goer. After Sunday Silence won the Kentucky Derby, the two hooked up in one of the most memorable races of all time, the 1989 Preakness. "I underestimated Sunday Silence that afternoon," Day said, "his recuperative ability. He had to check off a horse's heels going into the far turn, and we went on past him. I anticipated he'd come back down the stretch somewhere, but an eighth of a mile later, boom, there he was. Tremendous athletic ability. He ran around the turns like a hoop around a barrel. I had just let Easy Goer take a breather, and then when I saw Sunday Silence coming I tried to fire him up, but they got the jump on us. A great, great stretch run.

"I've always felt that Easy Goer was the better of the two, but the record doesn't bear that out. (Easy Goer won the Belmont Stakes over Sunday Silence, but was defeated a neck by his rival in the Breeders' Cup Classic later in the year.) But it was great fun. I wish it would have been 3-1 in our favor, but so it goes."

As with any rider, winning a Kentucky Derby was always a dream for Day, and he had come so close, finishing second three out of four years in a row going into 1992's running aboard Lil E. Tee. It was his tenth try in the Derby. "Each time was very emotional, and continues to be. I ride out on the racetrack and they play 'My Old Kentucky Home' and I get goosebumps and a lump in my throat and a tear in my eye. And if I ever get to where I don't feel that way, I'm gonna quit.

"When Lil E. Tee charged to the front and we neared the finish line and the realization set in that I was in fact going to win, it was a feeling that started way down deep inside. They say the longer you wait the sweeter the taste, and it was all in God's good time. It was way, way above my wildest expectations. I'd come so close, and thought I had a handle on what it would be like to win. Wrong. Wrong. Wrong."

Trainers such as Walden credit Day's patience as a key factor in the rider's success in major races.

"He brings such patience, and that's why he's been so successful in the Classics and in the Breeders' Cups," said

SKIP DICKSTEIN

Day's customary salute after a winning ride.

Walden of Day, who has captured three Belmont Stakes, five Preaknesses, and twelve Breeders' Cups. "Those are tense moments and energy-packed days, and he doesn't let the circumstances get to him. Even the best riders on those days have a tendency to move too soon, and Pat rides like he does every day of the week. He has a knack for getting a good trip. Certain riders do that by coming around other horses. Pat will save as much ground as possible."

Day feels a responsibility to save more than just ground in the racing industry. He has been active in the racetrack chaplaincy program around the country, which gives backstretch workers in particular a place to go for help or healing. Day works actively with disadvantaged children near his Louisville home because "we're supposed to uplift and encourage one another and be generous and helpful. And 'generous' doesn't just mean writing a check; it means with your time and your talents. So I consider it a privilege to help somebody or bring a smile to somebody's face and brighten their day."

Now closer to the end of his career than the beginning, Day has learned to savor each victory and appreciate the part played by many people behind the scenes. "I have greater respect for the grooms and the hotwalkers and the exercise people and the assistant trainers and the pony people at the gate. I get a lot of the accolades, but in truth we're like a chain and we're only as strong as the weakest link.

"At some point in time I realize God is going to call me into another arena. I don't know if that will be today, tomorrow, next year, or in ten years. If it's God's will that I should surpass Shoemaker and Laffit and be the leading rider in the country, Hallelujah. But if tonight on my way home God says, 'Pat, I want you to go to south Louisville and open up a mission for the homeless (he makes a whistling sound), I'm heading south, and that will be it."

Right on Time

In a dog-eat-dog world, Eddie Delahoussaye is top cat. While his peers grind away at one another, grabbing each other's mounts, reaching for the golden ring, the easygoing Cajun glides among them, collecting more than six thousand wins without the standard self-promotion and backbiting. He thrives on his wits and a better race plan, letting his colleagues think they have the upper hand. When crunch time arrives, however, there is Delahoussaye, swinging his horse to the outside and blowing past the field, leaving the others to wonder what hit them. On silent cat's paws, the top cat rides.

Patient on horseback and in life, Delahoussaye learned well from a half-century of experiences that began in New Iberia, Louisiana. If he has an enemy, it's nobody he's met. Yet gamblers certainly misunderstand Delahoussaye when they mistake his legendary patience for indifference. And so did the horsemen who downplayed his medical problems as a lack of intensity and took their business elsewhere. But "Steady Eddie" shrugs it all off and continues to win, despite not getting deep into the top barns.

"Loyalty goes two ways," he explained. "I've done a lot

of people a lot of favors, but I can count on one hand the number of people who have stayed loyal. There's a lot more of them I thought were really loyal who wasn't. But that's all right. That's life."

Life began for Delahoussaye, like it has for so many other talented jockeys, in rural Cajun country, where farmland predominates and horses are a big part of the culture. The farmers would "match races" on weekends. Parents would take their young children, and the kids would get curious about the animals.

Eddie Delahoussaye, born in 1951, was all of three when he first sat atop a horse. As a result, he was never afraid of them. At seven he was riding in horse shows. There were saddle horses, then Quarter Horses. An uncle trained some cheap runners, and a cousin was a jockey. At ten Eddie started riding match races. "I took a lot of spills and jumped a lot of fences, had a few head concussions, and I kept at it like an idiot. But I was passionate about it, I fell in love with it, and after forty years I'm still here."

It's one thing to fight weight as a top-class rider maintaining a career; it's quite another to have to do it as a kid. The owners or trainers who matched races wanted the lightest kids they could get for their horses. Delahoussaye tipped the scales at all of sixty-five pounds when he started riding. One day his father matched a race with another man. "My dad said to me, 'You gotta lose a couple of pounds.' And I said, 'What? I can't lose a couple of pounds — I'm ten years old.'

"They gave me a salt bath with hot, steaming water, like a Jacuzzi before they even had Jacuzzis," said Delahoussaye. "Too bad I wasn't smart enough, I coulda invented something. Then they put me in a sweat suit and put me in a hot room with a heater on. I pulled a coupla pounds but I was lightheaded. It really zaps you and takes the potassium out of you. But I'm ten, and I couldn't even spell 'potassium.' That was the first and last time I did that."

The match races were all straight sprints, some as short as thirty-six feet, others going out to one furlong, an eighth of a mile. Speed was king, as it was when Eddie D., as he is universally known, got to Evangeline Downs, where all Louisiana riders cut their teeth. Quarter Horses and Thoroughbreds ran at the same meeting.

The light went on in Delahoussaye's head when he rode the Thoroughbreds. "With Quarter Horses there's no strategy. You just go and keep them straight. Anybody who can sit on a horse can ride a Quarter Horse. But the Thoroughbred, the longer races, I fell in love with that. I wanted the strategy part, to see if I could use my mind. That was for me."

From Evangeline, Delahoussaye graduated to Fair Grounds in New Orleans. Soon he realized that most of the guys he was riding against were aggressive. He concentrated more on being patient, using the pace to his advantage and strategizing. Because film had just been introduced, the races weren't as roughly ridden as they had been, but there were still lessons to be learned, and veteran riders such as R.L. Beard and Ray Broussard to teach them.

"Bobby Beard was a speed rider who wouldn't let you in on the rail for nothing," said Eddie D. "I had just lost my apprentice bug and was riding against Bobby. I was in behind his horse and I was in trouble. I couldn't hold my horse. He looked back at me two or three times before he finally let me through. He told me afterwards, 'Eddie, if I hadn't seen how much trouble you had, no way I would have let you through. But I didn't want to drop you.' I was fortunate. Riders holler all the time, but back then you could holler all you want and they wouldn't let you through.

"Today riders tend to ride the horse the way it should be ridden, and if the best horse wins, the best horse wins. And that's the way it should be. Don't get me wrong — if you can race-ride, that's a different story from rough-riding. You've got to do your job. Back in those days they'd rough-ride you a little bit."

In a field where so many fall into this trap or that vice, Delahoussaye managed to remain "Steady Eddie." He credits his aunt, who helped raise him while his mother was battling illness, with showing him the value of a dollar early on. Under her guidance, he put the first dollar he earned in a match race in the bank for later. Brought up in a poor family, he learned the importance of saving.

"My first few years riding I wasn't doing that well, but I was still making some money and saving it. Unlike most riders, I began doing better when I lost my apprenticeship. Everybody said, 'Oh, you'll be dead once you lose the bug,' and I was saying, 'Dead? I'm dead now. I'm gonna be deader?' But I was raised the proper way. A lot of young people start in this game and make a lot of money, and they're not guided in the right way. They think it's gonna last and it doesn't, and then it's too late and they've lost a lot of it.

"You're young and naïve, and there's a lot of sharks out there — you get managers wanting to manage your money, and they steal from you. But it's hard to tell a kid who's winning big races that it's not going to last forever. Their egos and heads get too big. They buy a Mercedes and a house, and they got huge notes they're paying every month.

"We're not scientists or inventors of anything. We're

jockeys who go around in circles. It doesn't take much. We can be replaced. You can get hurt tomorrow and lose everything. You don't have a disability policy, which is very expensive. You get hurt, you'll lose your house and every- thing else. Kids should realize that."

From the late sixties until the late seventies Delahoussaye rode the circuit that rotated from Fair Grounds to Keeneland and Churchill Downs in Kentucky, and up to Arlington in Illinois and the New York tracks. Although he enjoyed steady success, several issues con- spired to send him West. At the time New York was more stringent in its scale of weights than was California, and weight was always an issue for Eddie D. He believes his career would have ended prematurely had he remained in the East.

Delahoussaye says keeping his weight down has been the biggest challenge of his career. Even in the beginning, he would reduce vigorously by taking the diuretic Lasix without knowing the side effects. In the long term the drug can cause problems with the heart, liver, and kidneys. "Like everybody else, I was ignorant about those things back then," he said.

Delahoussaye's battle with weight parallels that of Laffit Pincay's. Nutrition received much less attention than it does today, and it took riders a long time to learn how to manage their weight properly. In the mid-eighties, Delahoussaye, then a social drinker, realized that alcohol affected his weight and would end his career. He gave it up, changed his diet, and began exercising more. He's used to the discipline now, but admits that mentally it can be a drag. "You see peo- ple having a nice steak and you know as you get older and your metabolism slows down, you can't work it off. It gets harder, and you work more on the treadmill or the bike or with weights. I can't pull more than a pound in the hot box or it drains me. The statistics say I should weigh 145." Instead, Delahoussaye weighs in at 116 pounds.

Delahoussaye also had family concerns that figured in his move to California. Eddie and his wife, Juanita, a Mississippi native whom he met when both were in their teens, had a second child, Mandy, who was born in 1975 and was developmentally delayed. "There were better schools for her out in California," Delahoussaye said. "Back then we didn't know how bad a situation it was going to be, and there was an opportunity that maybe we could get help out there. And it was a way to stay put, rather than traveling around on the circuit back East. There was no way she could get an education doing that."

One of Delahoussaye's first big wins in California was in the 1980 Hollywood Gold Cup. The horse's name? Go West Young Man. California proved to be the final course in Delahoussaye's riding education. When he walked into the jocks' room in 1979, he found waiting for him Laffit Pincay, Bill Shoemaker, Chris McCarron, Don Pierce, Fernando Toro, and Darrel McHargue. "I can remember a reporter asking me if I'd have problems riding with these riders. Hell, these are the best in the world; how can you have problems with them? They know where they're at at all times. That's the kind of riders you want to ride with. I was in my glory."

Delahoussaye watched and learned. By studying how each individual rode, he learned when the other guy had horse beneath him and when he didn't. He began picking up on other riders' strategies and figured out how to apply his own patience. To watch Eddie D. ride is to realize why the casinos make money on blackjack. You let the other guy make the first move.

"I learned that from Shoemaker," said Eddie D. "In the early eighties he must have beat me a dozen times by a head or a nose. He was playing games with me. It took me awhile to figure it out, and after I did the tables were turned. Not that I beat him all the time, but I started to get there. You wait for the other guy to tip his hand. Every top rider, every patient rider knows exactly how much horse they have. Sometimes you can watch me and I'm not moving, but I have horse. It's cat and mouse, and I love the game. Love it."

While Delahoussaye's patience is often an asset during races, off the track it didn't always serve him well. Eddie was leading the riders' standings at Hollywood Park shortly after arriving in California, but his agents weren't doing quite as good a job as their client. "I was just a young kid, and I didn't focus much on the business end. One agent stopped showing up, and he was giving my business to someone else and spinning me," Eddie D. said. "I got schooled pretty good, but part of it was my fault. I'm an easygoing guy and let things ride and let them ride, and then you reach a point where you can't take it. But I was always doing good riding."

California provided a steady base for Delahoussaye's family, and the schools gave daughter Mandy the extra attention she required. Delahoussaye credits Mandy with teaching him about responsibility. His sister Roseanne has lived with him, Mandy, Juanita, and their other child, Loren, since the move to California, and has been invaluable in helping them with Mandy and doing Eddie's books as well.

"People who don't have handicapped kids naturally can't comprehend what it entails," said Delahoussaye. "Some people who have them can't handle it. Fortunately, we can handle it. Taking care of someone who needs help makes you closer as a family and makes you realize what life's all about. You want to win races and make a living, but winning's not everything. It's not easy. But we try to do everything together. If a person can have healthy kids, they're blessed. That's the richest thing in the world."

There is no pretense to Delahoussaye, no pauses while he searches for answers that would be politic or unrevealing. That is the way he is as a person and as a professional. Nobody around the track has a bad word to say about him, at least not one founded in fact. But because he doesn't entirely play the glad-hand game, Delahoussaye does not get his share of top mounts. If he's in a classic or Breeders' Cup race in the new century, almost invariably it's on longshots.

"People ask me why I'm not riding for the big outfits," he said, with no hint of malice in his tone. "Look, I'm forty-nine years old. I've been there, I've seen it. I don't want the hassle of these big-ego guys. If they want to ride me, they'll ride me. At this stage of the game, I'd rather ride for guys who are horsemen and enjoy the sport and try to do it the right way.

"The guys with the big egos and the big money behind them help the sport, but to me they're not true horsemen. Not from where I come from. They're promoters, they get the people with the money, they hire good help, and then it's just through numbers that they succeed. It's not from going to the barn and rubbin' on them horses."

Delahoussaye's career, while steady, reveals a definite pattern: His wins in five Triple Crown races and his seven

Breeders' Cup triumphs all occurred in or prior to 1993. That year he won Breeders' Cup races aboard Hollywood Wildcat (Distaff) and Cardmania (Sprint). The year before, he'd captured another pair with A.P. Indy (Classic) and Thirty Slews (Sprint). Risen Star had brought him Preakness and Belmont Stakes glory in 1988. And he became just the second rider since 1902 to win consecutive Kentucky Derbys when Gato Del Sol (1982) and Sunny's Halo (1983) won the roses.

His riding skills didn't suddenly fail him, but his health did. In 1994 Delahoussaye began experiencing sinus pain that prevented him from traveling. Being one of those problems most people don't experience or understand, owners and trainers misconstrued Delahoussaye's aversion to travel as disinterest in his mounts. "It's not that I didn't want to go ride for them," he explained. "I just couldn't fly. They misunderstood that. I was doing them a favor by not going when I was sick, riding a bad race, and costing them money. It hurt my business tremendously."

One day at Santa Anita, Delahoussaye was pulling up a horse after a race and began getting dizzy, almost blacking out. He thought he was dying. Four doctors failed to find the problem. Then trainer Bobby Frankel sent him to a blood specialist. Eddie's blood turned out fine, but X-rays revealed a polyp in his sinuses. After the operation it took another two years for the condition to finally settle down. Now he is healthy and traveling again, and business is steady, if not spectacular.

As Delahoussaye's health returned, his wife began having troubles of her own. In the summer of 2000, Juanita underwent frightening surgery to remove an aneurysm just below the skull near her brain. Had that aneurysm burst, she would not have survived. Today Juanita is doing great, although another aneurysm was found on the other side of her head. She is monitored, and doctors don't want to touch that one if they can avoid it.

Steady Eddie, though, rides on. He has not made the waves or public impression of Pincay (9,000-plus wins), Shoemaker (8,833), or McCarron (7,000-plus), but his 6,000-plus victories are not exactly chopped liver, considering his laid-back attitude toward his profession. While other riders have aggressively hustled up the best mounts for the top races through the years, Delahoussaye never drove himself to get every prime assignment. Instead, he worked with what came to him and let his agents try and handle the rest of it.

A triumphant Delahoussaye at the 1993 Breeders' Cup.

"I always want to be on top and be the leading rider," he said. "But I never wanted to go after it. It's hard enough work trying to focus on what you're doing in the afternoon without, 'God, I gotta get on this top horse, I gotta get on that top horse.' And I've seen a lot of guys do it and get to the top, but it made them miserable. And then the next meet would come along and they kinda went down. I guess that's why they call me 'Steady Eddie.' "

Play word association with any racetracker and his reaction to "Delahoussaye" will be "come-from-behind" rider. California race-caller Trevor Denman often punctuates Eddie D. victories from off the pace with "another patented ride from Eddie Delahoussaye." The rider himself, probably happy for any recognition, takes the label good-naturedly, but also makes it clear that's not the only way he knows how to win. "I love speed horses," he allows. "I'd rather have a horse with natural cruising speed than any horse who comes from behind, because a horse with speed you can put anywhere and do anything you want.

"A lot of people in California pegged me as a come-from-behind rider, but if you look at my charts going back to the Midwest and East, you'll see I can do it any way. California is such a speed-bias place that people think if you're not one-two-three leaving the gate, you're not going to win any races. Well, I've proven they're wrong about that. I think my style is just patience, and knowing the horse. Even Jerry Bailey told me a couple of years ago that 'I can't wait as long as you can.' Coming from him, that's a pretty good compliment."

Not every comment launched Delahoussaye's way is complimentary. Nothing incurs the wrath of gamblers more than betting a horse that never gets into the race.

They tend to forget the miracle finishes from behind when faced with a horse that is slow getting out of the gate. Always there must be a scapegoat. Often it is the rider, and Delahoussaye is one they love to grouse at. Eddie admits that the criticism got to him when he was younger, but now it "doesn't faze me because I know what I'm doing." Of course, gamblers can't see when horses aren't standing straight in the gate, nor would they know when the trainer instructs the rider not to send the horse.

The record speaks for itself. Delahoussaye has won just about every major race there is: the Big 'Cap, the Santa Anita Derby twice, the Malibu, the Hollywood Gold Cup three times, the Hollywood Futurity, the Pacific Classic, the Eddie Read Handicap four times, the Whitney, the Suburban, the Kentucky Oaks, the Jockey Club Gold Cup, the Coaching Club American Oaks, the Spinster, two Belmont Stakes, the Preakness, and, of course, back-to-back Kentucky Derbys, a feat accomplished just three other times, by Isaac Murphy, Jimmy Winkfield, and Ron Turcotte.

If anything put the cherry on top of Eddie D.'s Hall of Fame career, it was the 1982 and 1983 runnings of the Derby. Just for balance, one was front-running, the other that "patented" Eddie D. ride from the rear. He showed, once and for all, he could do it either way. Delahoussaye remembers having watched Shoemaker win the Derby on Lucky Debonair when the young Cajun was riding match races in his home state. "I'd love to be there one day," he thought.

He had high expectations entering the gate aboard Gato Del Sol. Before the race he told trainer Eddie Gregson, "Watch. If things set up, we'll wind up winning." After an unbelievable ride in which Delahoussaye wove his way from dead last through the field of eighteen other competitors, the trainer admitted, "Dang, you called it right on the head."

The following year was a whole different story with Sunny's Halo, except for the result. Delahoussaye put the colt on the lead and dared anyone to catch them. Chris McCarron and Desert Wine came calling at the top of the stretch. "Chris came up to me, but I had a lot of horse, and he seen it too," Delahoussaye remembered. "It's fun when you have horse at the head of the stretch and you're in front or laying second and these other guys are riding and you're just sitting. I said, 'Well boys, you all in trouble

Delahoussaye and A.P. Indy, the best he's ridden.

today.' I uncocked my stick and hit him twice and he rebroke, and that was the greatest feeling in the world."

His most memorable rides, however, are not necessarily the classics. A Letter to Harry, who was a multiple stakes winner in the seventies in the Midwest, stays close to Eddie's heart. The horse, a stalker, found himself on the lead in the 1979 New Orleans Handicap, running as slowly as possible. The other jockeys, realizing there was no pace on, came rushing past him at the five-eighths pole, and Delahoussaye dropped six lengths off them, watching the parade go by. He began creeping back up on the leaders, and at the quarter pole he was the only one who had horse left. A Letter to Harry won by five. Delahoussaye is the guy other riders least want to see when they look in the sideview mirrors of their peripheral vision.

"I loved the 1980 Masquette Stakes in New York when I beat Genuine Risk with Bold 'n Determined. I knew I had to save every inch I could. I was laying second and Jacinto Vasquez was laying fourth, and he came around me at the three-sixteenths pole and opened up a neck. But I could see he wasn't going any faster so I just sat and waited till the last thirty yards. I came back on and got her by a nose. And I heard LeRoy Jolley (Genuine Risk's trainer) went nuts, so that was a great thrill that day. LeRoy was a helluva horseman but he had a temper, and if things didn't go right he'd tell you. That was good just to lay it on him. I had the horse every step of the way, but I knew if I didn't time it right she was gonna come back on. And two jumps past the wire she was back in front of me."

There was the 1993 Breeders' Cup Distaff at Santa Anita, when Delahoussaye and Hollywood Wildcat were nose and nose with the great Paseana. Down the stretch

Eddie lost his stick. "I thought I was going to have a heart attack. I lost my composure. Looking back, I don't think she could have run any faster. But in a million dollar race, if I'da lost, I'd have never lived it down. I was slapping at her, screaming, doing everything. The only thing I didn't do was jump off." They won by a nose.

The best horse he's been on, in his opinion, was fellow Hall of Famer A.P. Indy, on whom he won the 1992 Belmont Stakes and Breeders' Cup Classic. Overcoming bad feet and an undescended testicle that bothered him, A.P. Indy was named Horse of the Year in 1992. "He was something special. We'll never know, but I think he'd have been a Triple Crown winner (he was scratched the day of the Kentucky Derby with a quarter crack). I took off some pretty good horses to go north and ride him in his first allowance win at Bay Meadows. If he had had any kind of feet, there's no telling what kind of horse he'd have been."

Delahoussaye now enjoys going to sales and picking out horses. He doesn't want to work the twenty-four-hour days required of a trainer, but once he retires from riding, he'd like to work as a bloodstock agent who "tries to guide people the right way. It's gonna be hard to change the reputation of the job, because bloodstock agents have done their damage," he acknowledges. Like with riding, the patient man is taking his time to learn and do it the right way in another trade.

"I've never blown my horn," he said, "but after riding with Laffit and Shoemaker, and with what I've learned, I don't want to say I'm a great rider. But I'm as good as any rider around this country." And as good a man.

7

KENT DESORMEAUX

Growing Pains

Trainer Roger Stein, whose weekend radio shows on Thoroughbred racing are popular throughout Southern California and the West, offered rider Kent Desormeaux the chance to come on his show one day in the mid-nineties to apologize for several riding gaffes. Bettors had grown incensed that too often Desormeaux became disinterested once he realized he couldn't win a race, and cost them place, show, and exotics money because he didn't persevere with mounts.

Desormeaux, though, hadn't yet reached a stage of maturity to deal properly with the criticism.

"He said, 'I can't believe you're doing this for me (putting me on your show),'" Stein remembers. "We went over some points before the show about how he realizes people are wagering and he doesn't mean to mess up and it won't happen again. Then we get on the air and I said, 'Kent, a lot of people are disappointed because they bet on these horses and you stand up early and the horse finishes fourth instead of third.' And he says, 'If they think it's so easy, they oughta come here and try it.' My jaw hit the floor. I didn't know what to say. He did everything but say, 'Screw them.'"

Desormeaux' attitude often overshadowed his compe-
tence as a rider at that point in his career. His retort to
Stein's question underscored that the path to the top of a
profession is often fueled by traits both good and bad. For
all the determination and single-mindedness success
requires, sometimes stubbornness and an inability to listen come along for the ride. Talent often carries with it
cockiness. An ease with words comes with not knowing
when to keep quiet.

Meld all those ingredients together into a spicy Cajun
stew, simmer it good and long, until the disparate elements
join together into a savory treat, and you'd have one Kent
Desormeaux.

The thirty-one-year-old colorful Cajun with the two-
hundred-watt smile generates some of the industry's best
quotes. A game horse "laid his life on the line for me." A
fast one "ran a hole through the wind." Another one ran by
other horses "like a train passing a hobo." Desormeaux
never met an audience he couldn't entertain, and his pat-
ter can cover a route of ground. He is as eager to talk as a
guy emerging from the wilderness who hasn't seen another human for a couple of weeks.

Along with the glib chatter comes marquee good looks
that have landed the rider jobs as a racing analyst and an
actor on the sandy and sexy television show *Baywatch*, in
which he played...a troubled jockey.

If life doesn't throw things at us until we're able to handle them, then Desormeaux' has taken a dramatic leap
toward enlightenment. Success came to him early, and
after departing almost as quickly, came back on again as
the wunderkind turned into a more mature veteran.
Professionally, his potential is unlimited. His four thou-

sand wins by age thirty (the youngest jockey to reach that plateau) attest to that.

Away from the track his grace and mettle have been impressive the past few years. The pressure and pain of parenting through the crisis of a child's disability, doing so with dignity, and the determination to knit his family ever closer have more than anything else marked the growth of Kent Desormeaux as a complete individual.

At points along the way, many would have quoted the odds of his progression as longer than those for a draft horse to win the Kentucky Derby.

Like so many other riders, such as Craig Perret, Eddie Delahoussaye, and Shane Sellers, Desormeaux hails from that fertile breeding ground of jockeys — the back country of Louisiana. In tiny Maurice, outside Lafayette, Kent was born the second of six children of Brenda and Harris Desormeaux. His older brother, Keith, today a successful Thoroughbred trainer, served as youthful competition to mark himself against, accelerating the younger brother's development.

The Desormeaux family owned a couple of horses that were kept on the property, and Harris also owned and operated a bush track in Lafayette called Akadiana Downs. On Sundays all kinds of breeds would come together to run thirty-five races and before, between, and after the races Keith and Kent would hold foot races against each other around the oval in non-pari-mutuel contests.

"Our family is very competitive and goal-oriented," Kent said. "Part of my mother's morals were that if you're going to do something, try to be the best at it or don't do it at all. That drive was instilled in us." Kent and Keith had horses they groomed and brushed and showed at 4-H Club events. They usually earned trophies.

119

"Kent was an excellent student and a tremendous athlete," remembered his mother, Brenda. "He played basketball, football, and baseball. He was quick as lightning, and he'd pray to God to make him tall because basketball was his favorite. Then he rode his first racehorse when he was twelve or thirteen and he decided he kind of liked that. He had tremendous athletic abilities, and he had the right size for that, and he could put his athleticism to use guiding the horse. He ended up asking God to forget all those prayers about getting tall."

God's greatest gifts are sometimes unanswered prayers, and so it worked out that Desormeaux found the avenue for

SKIP DICKSTEIN

The perks of fame: throwing the ceremonial first pitch for the Orioles during Preakness 2000 week.

his competitiveness and athletic prowess on the back of racehorses. He'd watched the Kentucky Derby on TV as a kid. "The first Derby I remember was Angel Cordero on...I don't even remember the horse. But I remember the call 'And down the stretch they come,' and the hair raised up on my back and from that day on I wanted to be a jockey."

The sixteen-year-old Desormeaux hit the Louisiana circuit, winning his first races and stakes at Evangeline Downs. But the inner drive wouldn't permit Desormeaux to stop and be satisfied with local accolades. Although still in high school and at the top of his class, involved with all sports and the student council, Desormeaux focused on one goal — becoming a jockey. He decided he needed to leave home to accomplish his dream in the grand style he envisioned.

"If that's why they make blinkers — to make someone focus — then I was wearing closed, full-cup blinkers," Desormeaux said. "I could see only the opportunity presented to me to move to Maryland. It was the opportunity I was looking for, and I left home with no second thoughts. It was 'Just go. Go baby go.'"

Other members of the family had plenty of second thoughts. "I thought leaving home was the biggest mistake he was ever going to make," Brenda Desormeaux said. "As a mother, I saw him going into medicine or law or something on that level. When he said he wanted to leave school and home, I was devastated, a tremendous heartbreak for me. I thought he was too young, but we didn't want him to turn rebellious on us. He'd made up his mind, and we had to let him go. With conditions."

Agent Gene Short had discovered Kent on the local circuit and taken him to Shreveport to fry bigger fish. Short guaranteed Brenda Desormeaux that Kent would live with him and his family up in Maryland. "I'm finding out now, much later, that Kent had a difficult time early on being away from his family. But he was never gonna let that on," Brenda said.

Desormeaux was likely too busy to be lonely for long. Fueled by that competitive nature and the drive to be the best, he led all jockeys with 450 victories in 1987, twenty of them coming in stakes, breaking Steve Cauthen's record for apprentices. Kent's mounts earned better than five million dollars that year, and the young rider received the Eclipse Award for outstanding apprentice jockey. The transition from Maurice to Maryland appeared seamless, but it wasn't.

"The biggest adjustment I ever made was moving from the bush tracks to the regular ones," said Desormeaux. "You go from no rules and regulations to being policed. As a kid you do things a certain way; then when you get to the real world you find out you're doing it the wrong way, that the rough stuff you're doing isn't even allowed. Those are tough barriers — you have to retrain the brain."

In 1989 Desormeaux and Short mapped out a plan that tested the boundaries of sanity. They set a goal of winning six hundred races for the year. "We could have written that movie *Planes, Trains, and Automobiles*," Desormeaux said, "because every day I was involved in one or all of the above. Races would end in Maryland, and I'd jump on a plane to make the card at the Meadowlands or drive up to Penn National or take the train to Garden State. There were days when I'd ride seventeen, eighteen horses and wouldn't win one and would want to quit. Then there were days when I won nine. It's like hitting that one good golf shot on the eighteenth after being frustrated all day. That one hole brings you back and you can't wait for the next day."

Poised at 598 victories in December, Desormeaux broke several ribs in a spill. His year was over two wins short of his goal, but the 598 were more than enough to smash Chris McCarron's previous record of 547, also achieved on the Maryland circuit. Desormeaux captured his first Eclipse Award as a journeyman and pocketed his third consecutive national victory title, joining Pat Day and Bill Hartack as the only riders to accomplish that triple bagger.

"Today I might not opt for such a strenuous routine, but only because a lot of my hopes and dreams as a jockey have been fulfilled," said Desormeaux. "I was just chasing the notion that it could be done, and I was trying to attain greatness. These were the steps toward that. Maryland presented a chance to build my credentials and eventually move on to the next town."

That gunslinger mentality pushed Desormeaux on. To be measured against the best, you have to compete against the best, so Kent gave up his dominant position in Maryland for a move cross-country to Los Angeles to tackle the powerful Southern California jockey colony. "I went from being the big fish in a small pond to barely even existing," he said. "In Maryland I rode ten a day, and it was a bad day if I didn't win three. In California I was lucky if I rode three, and that was tough to get used to."

He slowly began picking up mounts when the top riders left town for Breeders' Cup, Triple Crown, or major stakes races. Some stellar mounts fell to the brash young kid so used to success so early, and he was able to keep many of them. He seemed poised to blaze a trail to the top. All aspects of Desormeaux' life were clicking along.

He had married his childhood friend Sonia, also from Maurice. She remembers pinching his cheeks in school and telling him how cute he was. When they were kids, she had found him too full of himself; but he persevered, they married, and at the end of 1992 the couple was expecting their first child.

On December 11, while riding at Hollywood Park, a mount stumbled and dropped Kent to the track. Kicked in the head by a trailing horse, he fractured his skull in several places and had internal hemorrhaging. Doctors didn't think he would make it through the night, but they didn't know that Desormeaux determination. Battered, he still pulled through.

Four days later a distraught Sonia went into premature labor at a hospital across town. Despite being in still-precarious health, including deafness in one ear from the spill (his hearing in that ear has never returned), Kent demanded to be released from the hospital to be with his wife. Doctors decided to set him up next to Sonia in her room. Son Joshua was born nine weeks premature after a difficult delivery, after which Sonia became critically ill. Around Christmas all three were finally released to go home.

Six weeks after the spill, Kent beat all estimates for his return to racing and won with his first two mounts at Santa Anita. However, the whirlwind events of December 1992 made a lasting impression.

"You realize whether you win or lose it's not the end of the world," said Kent. "At the end of the day, if you have your health and your family...you realize they might be the only ones who still love you. To care for them and love them is more important than whether you got there first or not. And there's no one who desires to win more than I do. But if you don't, it's not the end of the world, and that was the most difficult thing I had to learn."

Whereas his personal life was growing in richness, Desormeaux' professional performance was coming under closer scrutiny in the mid-nineties. Desormeaux had drawn numerous fines and suspensions for failing to ride horses all the way to the wire. On several occasions he had stood up too soon, costing his mount a placing.

The low point came on November 28, 1993. Desormeaux had traveled to Japan to ride in the world's richest race at the time, the $3.6 million Japan Cup. Desormeaux, early in the card, rode three races on the same turf course that the main event would be run on. Yet, with Horse of the Year implications hanging in the balance for his mount, the Richard Mandella-trained Kotashaan, Desormeaux blundered the race away when he stood up in the irons one hundred meters from the finish. Realizing his mistake, Desormeaux went back to driving the horse, but it was too late, and Kotashaan finished second to Legacy World.

"I am truly embarrassed," he told reporters after the race. "It's not supposed to happen to a first-class rider. I can't apologize enough to the fans." But then, Desormeaux turned the incident into a "woe is me" riff. "It cost me money in purses and would have put me on the lead in earnings, which could have meant another Eclipse Award for me," he said. "That really hurts."

Both Desormeaux' performances and his mouth were hurting him. Back in the States, trainers were having to go to owners to make excuses for him. His brashness was no longer a positive, but rather one more in a growing list of negatives. He was on the hot seat. Business was drying up. It was time to grow up or get out.

"Whether I was right or wrong, I was wrong," Desormeaux said, looking back at that period. "If public perception was that I wasn't riding them out, then I wasn't. It didn't matter what I thought. That's what I had to learn. I trained myself to drive to the wire. They pay first through fifth, and until five horses pass me, I'll ask the horse for his life. Look, the man upstairs works in mysterious ways, and that was a lesson I had to go through."

While nobody questioned Desormeaux' ability, his mental state and maturity were other matters entirely. In the spring of 1997 Desormeaux and trainer Bob Baffert cut a deal. "I told him if he helped me get some of my two-year-olds ready, he could pick up mounts on some of them," Baffert recalled. One of those mounts was Real Quiet, a son of Quiet American whom Desormeaux piloted to victory in the Hollywood Futurity late in 1997. The narrow-bodied horse, nicknamed "The Fish" by Baffert, proved to be the tidal change in Desormeaux' career.

The pair finished second behind Indian Charlie, another Baffert charge, in the Santa Anita Derby in the spring of 1998. "We were a little behind schedule with the horse," Baffert said. "We didn't have him that sharp, and he also bled in the race. Also, Kent dropped his reins on the turn, then broke his stick. I told him afterwards he was lucky I had the winner or else I would have been like, 'What the hell were you doing back there?' "

Baffert kept Desormeaux aboard Real Quiet for the Kentucky Derby. "Kent has won a lot of races, and you want a guy who's been there," the trainer said. "Even though he had never won a Derby, he'd ridden a bunch of them. There's about ten top riders in the country you want in a big race, and Kent's one of them. He's upper echelon, and he's not going to panic much. That is a pressure, pressure situation. You know your ride's gonna be picked apart."

Don't believe anyone who tells you the Kentucky Derby is just another race. Today, Desormeaux can look back at his first Derby, aboard Purdue King in 1988, and remember everything, down to the paint chips on the starting gate. "It is very emotional coming onto that track. Very emotional," he said. "That first time I was overwhelmed. You are proud and excited to be there, and you feel like you've made it. Just being there was enough, and I was riding very hard so I wouldn't finish last."

Derby day in 1988 proved more emotional, as Desormeaux' grandmother passed away within hours of Kent's first Derby mount.

In 1990 Desormeaux rode to a third-place Derby finish with Pleasant Tap, who would go on to win an Eclipse Award as best older horse two years later. It was Kent's best Derby finish until he got aboard Real Quiet.

"I knew we had a good shot in the Derby that day, but I didn't want to get Kent nervous," Baffert said. "I told him that the horse was ready to roll, just get him down to the inside, ride the rail, sit behind a fast horse, and then you're on your own."

Desormeaux had seen most of the field close-up and felt Indian Charlie was the horse to beat. "I used him as a guide, keeping my eyes on him. When I peeled Real Quiet out at the three-eighths pole, he exploded, and I went by Indian Charlie like a train passing a hobo. The race was over right there. He was digging and really running, and I hadn't even asked him yet.

"Before I could raise my arm in joy, I was overcome with emotion and fell into tears. Two jumps later I was jubilant again. My whole career flashed through my eyes. I remembered breaking from the starting gate for the first time; traveling around the South with a horse named Skunk Him Up for Dale White; galloping horses in our backyard; days where I'd grab my grandfather's horse Rebel, put a saddle and bridle on him and race him down the gravel road and back home, all of ten minutes, take the saddle off him and cut him back loose in the pasture. That's how I learned to ride. I'd have to climb the fence to get on him, and before long he wouldn't stand next to the fence anymore, and I'd have to leap onto him. All of that went through my head when I hit the wire."

Desormeaux instantly understood the Derby triumph was a major marker in his career, and his life. Following the race he remembered his grandmother who'd passed away ten years before and how his mom was in Louisville with him that day to share the proud moment of his first Derby. He thanked his father for always having horses around. And then he talked about himself:

"I had some great success, and it all went to my head. I got a little too big for my britches, and it all fell apart. Now things are back in order."

After winning the Preakness and bidding for the Triple Crown, Desormeaux and Real Quiet, a horse purchased for a mere $17,000, became heroes. "I felt like I was the president of the United States," he said. After losing the Belmont Stakes by a nose, however, he felt like he was being impeached. "I was devastated. I had given my life to get there, and it didn't work out. I probably went too far in trying."

Some criticized Desormeaux for moving too soon with Real Quiet in the mile and a half Belmont. Baffert was not one of them. But he wasn't pleased with the jockey's tactics turning for home. "I had told him 'whatever you do, don't get your number taken down,'" said Baffert. "And then he went and pulled out in front of Victory Gallop. That upset me. He did it deliberately, and you can hurt a horse that way. Kent thought if he didn't do that then Victory Gallop would have blown right by him. He just didn't know his horse well enough. If he would have stayed where he was, Real Quiet would have kicked back on. The only time Victory Gallop was in front was the step at the wire."

Nevertheless, the Triple Crown trail and then riding top handicap horse Formal Gold reignited Desormeaux' career. He picked up winning stakes mounts on both coasts, piloting standouts such as Archers Bay, Ladies Din, Worldly Manner, Puerto Madero, Wild Rush, Keeper Hill, Labeeb, Fiji, and Excellent Meeting. He and conditioner Neil Drysdale started having steady success together, so

Desormeaux sitting pretty on Fusaichi Pegasus.

when Drysdale began pointing the highly touted Fusaichi Pegasus toward Churchill Downs for the 2000 Kentucky Derby, Desormeaux was on board.

"Kent is gifted, athletic, and he has a good rhythm," allowed Drysdale. "Horses relax well for him. He's got good hands. He was prepared to take his time with Fusaichi Pegasus and not rush him. Throughout the spring he rode the horse with patience. Then again, it might have been he didn't have a lot of options. He gave the horse a lovely ride in the Derby."

Fusaichi Pegasus, a notorious rabble-rouser leading up to the Derby, and his jockey picked the right day to showcase their enormous abilities. Weaving through the field from near the back of the pack, Desormeaux rode a race as brilliant as his mount's talent. But the experience was much different from the win two years before. "This time the whole race seemed like it was in slow motion," Desormeaux said. "The last time (he snaps his fingers), that's how long it took. As we went through the race this time, a situation would arise, and it seemed like it took five minutes to react to it, probably because I had a lot of horse and I'd been there already.

"But afterwards I had the same feeling inside. It just happened that this time I was on a horse who had antics. I figured if I dropped my hands and went to hootin' and hollerin' like a monkey, he might make a U-turn and I'd go straight. I didn't want to chew on sand, but inside I felt I'd accomplished a good ride and I was as jubilant as ever."

And more mature than ever. The apprentice wonder boy, in fourteen years, had climbed to the top, stumbling at times, but picking up himself, and valuable experience, along the way. "I've learned that if you want to be number one, it's not always how you ride out there, it's also how you conduct yourself. The stuff out on the track now, that's like riding a bike. But smiling when I don't feel like smiling, entertaining the owners and trainers when I don't feel like being there, those are the days you have to concentrate the most. When you're having a good time, it comes naturally. But when you're not, you'd better act like you still want it bad. That's what you learn in fourteen years."

Just when it seemed the strain from the pursuit of excellence was easing off Kent Desormeaux, another personal crisis hit. In 1999, Sonia went into early labor again with her second pregnancy, resulting in an emergency C-section. Their second son, Jacob, was born deaf. In November 1999 doctors performed a cochlear implant, putting near Jacob's ear a receiver of electrodes that would transmit sounds to the brain, in effect, building an ear. That implant was defective, and Jacob had to go through the surgery all over again.

Through this all, Desormeaux remained steady. He was patient with well-wishers and the press, even though there came a time when he wanted to stop talking about his son, particularly when there was no progress. But following the second surgery, Desormeaux reported that Jacob was responding to sounds such as dog barks and airplanes. "These are anxious, scary times," he said. "But my wife and I have never been so much in love. And my kids, I've never known them so well."

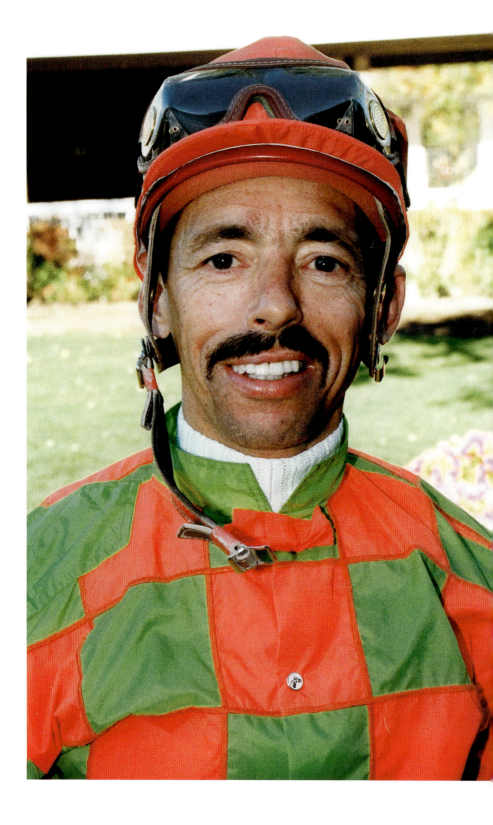

8

MARK GUIDRY

It's All Lagniappe

Because these pages chronicle the elite jockeys of the day, it is easy to forget that just a handful of the thousands of working riders win a Triple Crown or Breeders' Cup race. The overwhelming majority compete for low wages at small tracks, trying desperately to carve out a living. For each famous jockey, there are legions whose names will never grace headlines or whose faces will never be seen in televised winner's circle ceremonies.

And then there are some, like Mark Guidry, who fit between the extremes of stardom and anonymity. The affable Cajun didn't get to ride in his first Kentucky Derby until the age of forty. By forty-two he had ridden in a total of three Breeders' Cup races, despite being the leading jockey on the Chicago circuit throughout the 1990s. Just as he once left his native Louisiana to fight the larger battles, in 2001 Guidry ventured from the comfort of his Chicago success to try and make his mark in Florida, Kentucky, and New York.

He's had his successes, though not more than his share. He's still under the radar of national recognition and prominence. He's not the first or third or fifth name that comes to high-powered connections when they're looking for a big-race rider in an important graded stakes. And while he's looking to change that, Guidry freely admits his worst wounds have been self-inflicted. Yet at nearly 4,200 wins and counting, he is an accomplished rider with a winning personality.

Among the usual quiet of a jocks' room, where the norm is silent preparation or vacant stares at the television set, Guidry is a whirlwind of fresh air. He takes his business seriously, but his presence lights up the room. He makes travel plans to get from Northern Kentucky's Turfway Park to Ellis Park in the western part of the state, figuring out how to stop along the way at another jockey's house for a home-cooked meal. When a rider pops his head in and out of a window trying to disrupt an interview, Guidry asks if he's crazy. "I didn't mean anything by it," the jock says, defensive for a moment. "Man, you don't need to explain yourself to me," says Guidry, lightening the moment.

Guidry was the lone boy among six sisters in his home in Lafayette, Louisiana, the same area that produced Kent Desormeaux and Corey Lanerie. He is kin to former New York Yankees pitcher and Cy Young Award winner Ron Guidry. (Whereas the hurler was known as "Louisiana Lightning" for his fastball, the rider took the nickname "Louisiana Laser.") His mother came from a farming family, and Mark's uncles had racehorses. Guidry's dad was an electrician, and the family struggled to make ends meet. But his father loved to ride pleasure horses on weekends, and an uncle gave Mark a Shetland pony named Cheyenne, who became dear to him. "That was my only transportation, I didn't have no bicycle," Guidry remembered. "I started riding that Shetland when I was four. Didn't waste no time with a saddle — I'd just put the bridle on him every afternoon and ride.

"I started riding him in horse shows. We went everywhere together. When my dad had to work evenings, my mom would hook up the truck and trailer and bring me to the horse shows. When she couldn't bring me, all the kids in the area would meet up and ride to the shows, riding back past midnight in the dark along gravel roads." Guidry was six at the time.

Two years later he graduated to a half-Shetland, half-Quarter Horse named Chico. Guidry rode down the road to trainer Anatole Bourque's farm, where he cleaned stalls and brushed horses. He eventually made it over to the bush track at Tee Maurice, exercising the Quarter Horses that ran every other Sunday. "I told the trainer, I.V. Roy, that I wanted to ride, and he said, 'you don't even know how to come out the gate.' So I put my exercise saddle on Chico, and me and Chico would get in there and come out fifteen times. Three weeks later I was riding match races. I was nine."

After riding the straightaways for a couple of years, Guidry was taken by his dad to Carencro, a round track where Thoroughbreds raced. He fell in love with them and the atmosphere of the races. "When my daddy would bring me to the match races, I was watching Eddie Delahoussaye and Ray Sibille ride. The feel was kind of like Saratoga — they had the trees and we'd picnic and they got drunk all day and everybody had a good time and got along good, all them boys. Them trainers had day jobs and did their barn work in the morning and went to jobs and came back after. They were working their butts off just to pay for the feed, and they helped each other out. Even if you were green, they let you work because they couldn't afford to pay anybody else.

"Then the match races on the weekends all the boys came out, and whoever had the most money would race for the bigger purses — one hundred dollars, two hundred dollars on each side was a lot of money. I rode for ten dollars or twenty dollars on each side, and you had to chase the people down for the two dollars you was riding for. And you damn near wouldn't get it. There was no pressure — they was drinking all day long and making Calcutta pools on the other horses so by the time their race come it was like, 'what the hell.' That experience right there was worth a lot. I'll never be able to get them days back, and neither will anybody else. Something that went out with the dinosaurs. I was grateful to be born in that era. Nowadays I think they have one bush track left back home. There aren't the opportunities there used to be, and it's a shame."

What Cheyenne and Chico didn't teach him, Guidry picked up when he got to Evangeline Downs in Lafayette as a fifteen-year-old, ninth-grade dropout. He copied things from good gate riders, from riders with a lot of patience, and put it all together in his own package. He prides himself as a good judge of pace and received another of his nicknames, Doctor of Pace, at Evangeline. "I used to ride a horse who always came from left field and got out (bore out) so bad you had to ride him on the outside, name of Bear Adams. One night in the feature race we were rounding the turn, and I'm rolling on the outside and the announcer said, 'And the Doctor has the

Bear in high gear,' and that's stuck with me through the years because I like to come from behind. My wife has a few nicknames for me, but I don't think I want to get into that."

In 1974 Guidry rode his first official winner, at Evangeline, Tempermental Tom for Anatole Bourque, on whose farm he got his start cleaning stalls. All his fellow riders from the bush tracks were there with Guidry, and "getting initiated, it took me a week to get the Vaseline out of my hair because it was long and curly. We had seven or eight guys who had the bug (apprentice weight allowance) the same meet. We kept the bug rolling. The only difference from the bush tracks is we were changing our clothes at the track instead of wearing them there and riding. And we were getting paid, so that was all right. That kind of spoiled the hell out of a lot of us."

The ease with which riding, and winning, came to Guidry ended up hurting him, however, along with his headstrong attitude. He didn't have to put much effort into riding, and now admits he abused his skill. He was sixteen, riding all over the state, and "had my own head. I did what the hell I wanted. I was making the money and that was my attitude. I have a son today who has the same thing. It hurt me because then I got in with the wrong environment and the wrong crowd."

Guidry fell in and out of riding because he wasn't dedicated to it. When he got half a reason, or began battling weight, he quit and worked other jobs such as carpentry or in the oil fields on a derrick. "At the end of that day, or in the middle, I'd say, 'Man, riding is easier than this.' "

Much of his problem stemmed from the copious

amounts of drugs he was ingesting, chiefly cocaine. His own rebellious nature, coupled with the fact he was watching the older riders do drugs, made it a natural for Guidry, who makes no excuses and passes no blame for his behavior. "Back in the seventies when I started, that's how it was; that's what my idols did, and I wanted to be like my idols," Guidry said. "There was guys seeing pink elephants on the racetrack, and they were leading riders. That made it okay. My sisters all went to college and never tried anything. I quit school and was always the rebel of the family, and I lived up to it. I'm grateful it didn't kill me, because it damn sure could have. That was me, man. That's how I lived."

Guidry was a solid, if not spectacular, rider around Louisiana, settling for win percentages in the low- to mid-teens each year. Clearly his lifestyle was hindering his performance. So when he got the opportunity in 1987 to move north and begin riding at Fairmount Park near St. Louis, Guidry and his wife, Tina, who had two young children at the time, decided change might be good. After the move his win percentage shot up to seventeen percent, and his mounts earned $828,615 that first year, a major boost from the $200,000 range in Louisiana. Guidry began hitting Balmoral in Chicago, then Sportsman's Park and Hawthorne. He was riding Sportsman's during the day and Balmoral at night, and became leading rider at both places. But Guidry had not yet outrun his troubles.

"We started rockin' them and making money, but it was fueling my addiction pretty good to keep up the pace I was on. I was doing cocaine just to keep me going. I'd ride all day, catch a helicopter or drive a car to ride all night. By the time I got home it was 1:30 in the morning and I was up at 5:30. It all came to a head. It was destined to. I didn't think it was affecting my riding at the time, but looking back, it affected a whole lot. Put a lot of people in danger. You think you're real sharp, but you ain't too coherent and your thinking is not clear."

After a riding suspension in 1989, Guidry disappeared for a few days and family and friends filed a a missing-persons report. When he resurfaced, he went into "rehab and treatment, psychiatric and everything, the whole nine yards."

A hard-earned milestone for Guidry.

Oddly enough, when Guidry returned to riding after rehab, he experienced fear for the first time on horseback. "Everything was too clear," he said. "I realized, 'damn, this is pretty dangerous here.' I had to figure it all out again. Before I would just react. Now I was acting, riding in tight spots. It was really weird. I also realized I couldn't see well at night, so I got contacts, and everything got magnified.

"But me and my agent at the time, Dennis Cooper, worked our asses off. Nobody gave us anything. We worked for every damn thing we got, which made it a whole lot sweeter." What Guidry got was riding crowns at Hawthorne in 1990, 1991, 1994, 1995, and 1996. He was just as good at Sportsman's Park, winning crowns there in 1991, 1993, 1994, 1995, 1996, and 1997. He won the Arlington riding title in 1992 and 2000. His riding style fit nicely with the Chicago tracks that favor off-the-pace runners in general. And for the first time he gained control of his life — working and coming home, maybe dinner out with his wife.

Guidry began to hone the natural riding ability learned in his childhood, but without the destructive rebelliousness. He was still getting his kicks, but his quest for speed was now being satiated by fast vehicles — Harley-Davidsons and, recently, a new Corvette. His sobriety allowed his feel for horses to come to the fore. "I've been familiar with horses all my life. You can feel them and work with them. Especially them young colts, when they want to nut up with you — if you allow them to get you, they ain't gonna pay attention. But if you nut back up to them, and show them the right way right off of jump street, we all right then. If I got along with my kids as well as I do the horses, then everything would be fine."

In 1989 Guidry's mounts earned $1.6 million, and a year later the total climbed to $2.9 million. He claimed his first graded stakes win in 1990 when he piloted Black Tie Affair under the wire first in the grade III Commonwealth Breeders' Cup Stakes at Keeneland. Black Tie Affair would go on to win the Breeders' Cup Classic in 1991, but was a relative unknown when Guidry first partnered him. The horse became the rider's ticket to places he'd never before been. Guidry and Black Tie Affair went sprinting against the likes of champions Housebuster and Easy Goer.

"That's some nice horses to be around. And going to Belmont and Aqueduct — I never was out of Chicago except Fairmount or Delta Downs. In New York you're riding with boys that are Hall of Famers, everybody you look up to, and they're on each side of you in that gate. It was a little intimidating. Then the more you ride with them the more you get to know them and the easier it gets. Of course, they're still on the right horses and they gonna be there, but it's a lot different today."

Black Tie Affair passed from Guidry to Shane Sellers to Pat Day and then to Jerry Bailey, who won the Breeders' Cup with him. Guidry has absolutely no hard feelings when it comes to the game of jockey musical chairs, that is, getting taken off mounts. "I was tooken off Black Tie Affair, I was tooken off Buck's Boy after I rode him in the Breeders' Cup and he come back a year later and won it. I've been tooken off horses just like everybody else has. But I've also picked up a lot of horses they've taken others off of, so it works out. Only a select few get to pick and choose. The rest of us scratch and work and pray that we'll run second or third and hope the politics of the game don't take us off.

"You may get to the mountain top, but you can't stay there forever. It's a very humbling game. You gotta keep on a very even keel, because what's gonna go up is gonna come down. That's what makes this game so great. And when things start slowing down, they look for someone to blame. For owners it's the rider who's gonna go, then the trainer. Everyone's got somebody to answer to."

Black Tie Affair gave Guidry his first graded stakes win.

Although graded stakes wins for Guidry remained the exception rather than the norm (through New Year's Day 2002 thirty-five of his 180 career stakes wins were graded), he kept grinding out winners and purse money throughout the nineties. His mounts earned between five million dollars and six million dollars each year for much of the decade. Illinois champions like Coni Bug, Darley Dancer, and Galaxy Girl were his bread and butter. Count the Time won the Fairmount Derby and ran second in the Super Derby, "beat a zap by Senor Thomas. Can you believe the luck? And in front of my home crowd. Are you crazy? I was riding my ass off. So many horses came through at certain times — Megan's Bluff, Reno Rumble, so many came through when I needed them to and helped me get where I am today."

Guidry got to taste Breeders' Cup competition for the first time in 1997 at Hollywood Park, when he ended up with mounts in the two grass races, Wild Event in the Mile and Buck's Boy in the Turf. "What a great experience," Guidry said, the excitement still not lost on him four years after the fact. "My first million-dollar races, and I thought I had a shot with both them horses. I told myself 'I'm gonna win both these races.' And how much that would have pole-vaulted my career. In the Mile I got to the rail, and there's ten horses strung out across the track. Jerry Bailey (on Geri) is in front of me three-quarters of a length and he's baby-sitting me all around the racetrack. He wants to drop over, but I'm in there just enough so he can't. And he's saying 'C'mon Gid' and I'm saying 'Nah, you ain't gonna get me outta this spot.' Finally we get to the last turn and there was nothing he could do anymore. They're coming over on him, and I had to take back a little bit and get out of there. So we run bad (ninth).

"Buck's Boy, man, it was such a great feeling to be on the lead going a mile and a half, and they didn't come get me 'til we were turning for home. I mean, God, it was good. Turning for home, I thought we could do it. Damn, it was emotional. He run fourth, and coming back I got tears in my eyes, upset I didn't win. Whenever I'm gonna quit bein' like that, I think I'm gonna give it up."

Three years later, when Guidry got the opportunity to ride in his first Kentucky Derby, the emotion was still in evidence. Even though he was on a longshot, Deputy Warlock, Guidry believed. "They had to beat him before they could tell me I wasn't gonna win that Derby," he said. "It was great just to be there. Man, I was like a kid. The Kentucky Derby is the dream. Coming out of that tunnel, I cried, all emotional, but once I got out on the racetrack, I was at home and it was okay. But getting to the track, 'My Old Kentucky Home' was playing and my mom and all my sisters, my wife, my kids, my friends are in the grandstand. It was a great feeling. I wouldn't trade it for the world." Deputy Warlock finished tenth.

Guidry returned to the Breeders' Cup in 2000 at Churchill Downs aboard Juvenile Fillies contender She's a Devil Due. Guidry and the daughter of Devil His Due were four for four heading into the race, including a stirring win in the Walmac International Alcibiades Stakes at Keeneland. She's a Devil Due was owned by Brian Griggs and Mike Goetz, two assistant managers at the Georgetown, Kentucky, Toyota plant. She was trained by Ken McPeek, whose wife, Sue, had undergone cancer surgery shortly before the Breeders' Cup.

"Out of all the horses I've ridden, she's probably my favorite," Guidry said. "She had more heart and determination — the harder I'd ride her, the harder she'd run. She really ran her heart out in the Breeders' Cup. Turning for home I was wide but we had momentum. I couldn't beat the filly in front (Caressing). I ran up to her and couldn't get her. But she was such a great trier. With Brian and Mike and what Kenny's wife was going through, it seemed like it was time, everything fit, but it just wasn't meant to be."

The taste of the big time must have suited Guidry. In 2001, he made the decision to leave his Chicago home and ride at Gulfstream Park in South Florida over the winter, Kentucky in the spring, and Saratoga for the summer. He had grown complacent in the Windy City and figured some new challenges would kick-start him. "I don't want to get down the road three or five years and wished I would have done this. I'm grateful for the goals I've reached, but there comes a time when you have to set different goals. I'd love to win a Breeders' Cup, a Derby, a Triple Crown race. I'd love to be a top five rider in the nation within the next couple of years. If I don't, then I tried, I did my best, and I can sleep at night knowing that."

So Guidry entered a new world. Instead of trainers in Chicago legging him up with a "good luck," now he has trainers who don't know him as well, who are giving him lots of instructions. He's had to prove himself all over again. "It keeps you sharp; it keeps you alert. It's a good thing," he maintains. "But on the other hand, I'm forty-two years old..."

Another problem was about to resurface in Guidry's

life. After twelve years of sobriety, Guidry slipped off the wagon. Not with cocaine. But he smoked some marijuana on a deep-sea fishing trip in Florida with friends. His timing couldn't have been worse. On March 24, 2001, Guidry climbed aboard a relative unknown named Balto Star in the Spiral Stakes at Turfway Park for trainer Todd Pletcher and the Anstu Stables of Stuart and Anita Subotnick. The Glitterman gelding romped on the front end by twelve and three-quarters lengths. The following day at Fair Grounds in New Orleans, Guidry's name came up for random drug testing.

The test came up positive for pot, and Guidry appealed, in effect keeping the news from going public until the appeal was heard. In the meantime, he carried the secret around, afraid to tell his wife, horsemen, even his agent. In April, Balto Star repeated his tour de force Spiral performance in the Arkansas Derby, punching his ticket for Churchill Downs the first Saturday in May. Guidry was terrified. He had waited so long for a Derby contender, and now he had one and didn't want to blow it with the drug positive. Yet his secret was exploding inside him. "It was stupid and I'm not going to defend what I did, but it wasn't like I was on a binge," he said. "I'm the same human being who won the Spiral, won the Arkansas Derby, I'm not no different. I made a mistake, I took a couple of hits, but I didn't want to be judged, and I sure didn't want to be taken off for the Derby. Can you imagine those headlines?

"Every day when the (*Daily Racing*) *Form* came out I would page through it in a panic. Every time the phone rang in the jocks' room, my hair would stand on end. I drove from Louisiana to Kentucky, and it was the longest trip I ever took. I wanted to die. I actually contemplated harming myself. I got to Turfway, and the priest that comes Sundays walked right across my path. I said to myself, 'Look at this.' So after the service I went to his room, closed the door, and he was the first soul I told about all this. He lightened me up, gave me strength, and told me I was only human. I stepped into the garden and took a bite of the forbidden fruit, and I had to pay for it. No way around it."

Guidry was able to come clean to a few key friends in the business. The goodwill he had built up through his personality came back to him now, giving him strength. But he did not tell the connections of his Derby mount. Instead, he buried himself in preparation for the first Saturday in May. He studied the past performances of every horse in the race for three days. "I knew everybody's colors. I knew who was gonna be where and when. And you know what? When the gates opened, ain't nothin' went like I thought it would. It just goes to show you, man. You never know."

Guidry and Balto Star pressed the hot pace set by Songandaprayer, staying in the race until the final turn, when the quick fractions took their toll on the frontrunners. Balto Star faded to finish fourteenth. Shortly after the Derby, Guidry gave up on his appeal and was set down for thirty days. "People were upset and disappointed, but my family and the racetrack people were very supportive for the most part. The racetrack is my family, too. These are my friends. Not acquaintances. I have a special relationship with everybody. I try to, anyway. Some people you just can't get along with."

Guidry returned to the races on Belmont Stakes Day in

early June. But not aboard Balto Star, who was ridden by Chris McCarron in the Belmont, and by Pat Day at Saratoga. Chalk up another mount that Guidry got "tooken off." Still, the Cajun came back strong. He was leading the Arlington Park meeting in early summer when he decided to tackle Saratoga instead, leaving behind a sure thing for tougher trails. "I accomplished more at Saratoga than I would have winning fifty more races at Arlington," he noted. "It was a big challenge. People told me if I won five over there I'd be doing good, so immediately I set my goal on ten. When I got to ten, I set my sights on fifteen. I got to twelve."

At the 2001-2002 winter meeting at Calder, Guidry excelled and earned the best winning percentage of all riders. He continued to hold his own riding against the 'big boys' at Gulfstream Park in early 2002.

Nearly forty years after first climbing aboard that Shetland pony, Guidry plunges on, still trying to make a name for himself. He realizes he's been his own worst enemy. Yet he also knows he's done pretty well for a dirt-poor kid from the Bayou who had little else but that pony. He remembers breaking his back in three places and cracking his skull in a fall in 1978 in Louisiana. "My whole ear was hanging off. Look, one of my ears looks like Mr. Spock's," he says, laughing. "I was on the track shakin' like a chicken. I thought I was dead. Yeah, I've been very fortunate.

"Not that many years ago I was driving a 'sixty-seven Plymouth Satellite all rusted out, didn't have no roof, and the seats were all torn up. I remember them days. I've been trying to make up for them. I've had a good career. Did a lot more than I ever thought I would. Four thousand wins?

For a guy who couldn't buy a loaf of bread? Hell, yeah, I think it's turned out pretty damn well. I'm very grateful, even if I never win another race. I've been blessed with a lot of things. This is all lagniappe; it's all gravy. That's what we call it back home. Lagniappe."

CHRIS MCCARRON

Thinking Man's Guide

I t would not be a major tout to proclaim Chris
McCarron by several lengths the most cerebral big-
time jockey. Among his reading interests are books on
sports psychology, from which he tries to gain an extra
measure of expertise to apply to his craft. One such work
described how the successful athlete must shift focus
between narrow- and broad-mindedness in a flash to
know everything that is going on around him and make
snap decisions in the heat of battle.

McCarron has turned his ability to see the big picture
into an art during a professional riding career that began
in 1974. Not only does he carry several battle plans with
him onto the racetrack, but also his focus carries well
beyond himself. Sure, he thinks about how to maximize
his own efficiency and skills; after all, it's not by accident
that McCarron's mounts have earned a world-record
$250,000,000-plus through the years.

But McCarron also thinks about changes that might be
good for his sport. He ponders the marketing successes
and failures of racing and other sports, solicits money year
in and year out to help his fallen peers through the Don

MacBeth Memorial Jockey Fund, and lends himself to numerous other charitable organizations.

He measures questions carefully, thinking before answering and wanting to be honest but not wanting to give away anything that would offend. He is far more anxious to promote riders as a professional group than he is any one rider in particular. He is, to put it scientifically, a good apple as well as a smart cookie.

As a jockey, he could almost be considered an assistant trainer. Although this is not every trainer's preference, the successful conditioners that use McCarron steadily, such as Ron McAnally, Jenine Sahadi, and Jay Robbins, swear by him. Others often swear *at* him, particularly when he is beating them in stakes races, which he wins at an admirable clip of twenty-one percent. In a celebrated incident at a press conference to hype the running of the 2000 Santa Anita Derby, trainer Bob Baffert turned to Sahadi and asked, "Who's training this horse, you or Chris McCarron?" Although most, Sahadi included, took the offhand comment as a dig at her, it could just as likely have been McCarron whom Baffert was attempting to tweak.

McCarron is a resource, if trainers choose to use him as such, who can measure what each horse wants to do and how it wants to do it. He remembers the habits of horses he's ridden and ridden against, and he possesses an almost paranormal feel for the animal. He is among the elite handful of jockeys to whom owners and trainers turn when they need a big performance.

His ability is all the more surprising considering McCarron didn't grow up around horses. His family lived in the Boston suburb of Dorchester, and McCarron kept busy playing whatever sport was in season, except for hockey, which he played on rinks and in the streets eight months a year. It was his older brother, Gregg, who introduced horses into the family. While working as a stock boy at a Jordan Marsh department store, Gregg was approached by a woman with racetrack connections who suggested his build was far better suited to riding horses than hauling boxes. Soon Gregg was at Suffolk Downs, learning the game at age nineteen. Younger brother Chris was sixteen when he first sat on a pony.

"When Gregg got going riding with the horses, I could see he was having fun, and the family would go to watch him," Chris said. "He taught me how to figure out how much money he was making, and it looked pretty good. So in 1971, before my senior year in high school, I got my first job hotwalking, at Rockingham in New Hampshire."

Odie Clelland taught the McCarron brothers the ins and outs of riding. The late trainer had become well known for bringing out young riders after his work with Eddie Arcaro, who went on to the Hall of Fame. Clelland instructed Arcaro before selling the jockey's contract to Greentree Stable.

McCarron attributes most of his early success to God-given physical ability as opposed to any great mental prowess. "If you don't have the physical talent to communicate with and get run out of the horses, most likely they're not going to run as fast as they can for you, and you're not going to win many races," he said. "And then you have the snowball effect — if you don't get winners you don't get more mounts, and if you don't get more mounts then the winners don't come."

The winners came in droves for McCarron right off the bat. Clelland usually left New England for New Orleans in the winter, but as he got older, he looked for a winter haven closer to home and settled on Maryland. McCarron, after graduating high school and under contract to Clelland, began riding as an apprentice on that circuit, which encompassed Bowie, Pimlico, Laurel, and Delaware Park. He simply had a way with horses. "I'd walk into the paddock being friendly to the trainers and owners — 'Hi, how are you doing?' — and get up on the horses, and they'd run like the dickens for me. I won 547 races that year — all on talent. I didn't know what I was doing out there. I had no savvy. I wasn't even close to being polished. It was physical ability."

It was the finesse that McCarron became famous for later that served him well from the beginning. Not known as a physical rider in the mold of Pincay, McCarron had the good sense to use that finesse on and off the track, educating himself to the other aspects of riding. Brother Gregg showed him how to read past performances, analyzing which horses possessed true, free-running speed and which were rank and spending themselves too early. McCarron was doing his homework.

"Clinton Pitts invited me into the film room every day to watch the films from the previous day at Pimlico," said McCarron. "So I watched nine races a day from every different angle; in essence, ninety races a day for sixty days. And I learned immediately how important it was to use anticipation in your strategy, to be able to see a sixteenth of a mile ahead of me. 'If I decide to do this now, here's what the result will be a sixteenth of a mile down the track.'"

Reviewing races is a habit McCarron has kept throughout his career. "If I can't remember how a particular horse runs, whether I'm riding him or riding against him, I'll go and refresh my memory by going into the video library, and I'll get an idea of how I want to ride the race. When I walk into the paddock and the trainer has his program marked 'speed, speed, speed,' I might say 'this horse shows speed on paper, but believe me, they've been sending him every time he runs. If they don't send him to the lead today, he won't be in the first flight.' And they look at me like, 'where'd you get that from?' "

McCarron's 547 wins in 1974 set a one-year record, one that stood until 1989 when another apprentice on the Maryland circuit, Kent Desormeaux, riding day and night in Maryland, Pennsylvania, and New Jersey, shattered it with 598 triumphs. McCarron's campaign brought him an Eclipse Award for top apprentice. He is one of only three riders,

McCarron and Alysheba survived an eventful 1987 Derby.

Desormeaux and Steve Cauthen being the others, who have won Eclipse Awards as both apprentices and journeymen.

McCarron's early success is notable for what it didn't bring him: trouble. While other riders handle early success and the sudden influx of money with the aplomb of sailors on leave, McCarron steered clear of rampant self-destruction. He admits that there were "periods of my career when I'd enjoy going out and having a party, the typical kid stuff and everything. But I never got myself into any trouble, and never allowed it to affect my performance or my business, and that comes from the way I was raised."

One of nine children, McCarron was brought up with strong family values. "We were devout Catholics and adhered to the basic philosophy of treating people like you'd want to be treated. That has kept me in good stead with my own family, my friends, and my business associates."

McCarron met his wife, Judy, when she got a job with Odie Clelland at the same time he did back in 1971. "We started at ground zero at the end of a shank," is how he puts it today. When Judy comes to the saddling paddock to support him now, Chris' eyes light up. They renewed their wedding vows upon their twenty-fifth wedding anniversary. The pictures of his three daughters fly out of his wallet at first mention of family. Erin lives in Florida and wants to be a marine biologist; Stephanie is in Northern California hoping to become a show-horse trainer; and Kristin is starting college.

McCarron's career moved up when he began traveling to Churchill Downs and winning stakes races there. Partnered with Sweet Alliance, he took down the Pocahontas Stakes in 1976 and then returned the following year to win the Kentucky Oaks and the La Troienne Stakes with her. In

1978 he captured the Louisiana and Arkansas derbys aboard Esops Foibles in early spring. By mid-May, he had shifted his tack to Southern California and won a pair of grade II races, the Will Rogers Handicap and the Lakeside Handicap, before the month was out. He has been a Southern California fixture since.

"Moving out there and the upward arc in regards to success, it's probably in my genes based on a competitive spirit I was raised with," McCarron said. "My dad was an extremely intense competitor, a good athlete. And Gregg, if you'd watch him on a basketball court, you'd think he was seven feet tall. He brought that attitude with him into his riding career, and I'd like to think I did as well."

By 1980 the percentage of McCarron's mounts that visited the winner's circle hit twenty-one percent, good enough to earn the rider an Eclipse Award. It was the first of eleven consecutive years that he won at twenty percent or better. The national average is eight percent. Even more impressive was his performance in stakes races. He won on twenty-four percent of his stakes mounts in 1981, and continued at better than twenty percent eight straight years. That number would have hit sixteen straight years if not for dipping to nineteen percent in 1989 and 1991. Also, the roster of his stakes winners began to be peppered with familiar names in the early eighties, when his partners included Flying Paster, Lord Avie, Wickerr, Stalwart, Jaklin Klugman, and Lemhi Gold.

On July 4, 1983, trainer Ron McAnally gave McCarron a leg up on John Henry, the 1981 Horse of the Year. The legendary gelding and McCarron won not only the American Handicap that day, but also the Hollywood Turf Cup in December. In 1984 they were together for victories in the

Golden Gate Handicap, the Hollywood Invitational Handicap, the Sunset Handicap, and the Budweiser Arlington Million at Arlington Park. John Henry's victory in the inaugural Arlington Million three years earlier had earned him legendary status when, in one of the most famous finishes in racing history, he came from nowhere to nose The Bart on the wire. The 1984 edition with McCarron was not so dramatic, as they defeated Royal Heroine by one and three-quarters lengths. One month later they captured the Turf Classic at Belmont Park, then closed out John Henry's remarkable career with a victory in the Ballantine's Scotch Classic at Meadowlands.

"We've been together a long time," noted Hall of Famer McAnally, who has put McCarron on countless horses, many of them top stakes runners. "He's probably one of the most intelligent riders we have. Chris remembers races and horses he's ridden and other horses in the race he's ridden. He comes by every morning and gets to know the horse he's riding. He works horses he hasn't ridden. He watches tapes of horses from their native countries. He has their interest at heart. If your mind is set that this is the job you want to do, and you concentrate on it and really get into it, you'll be a success at it. And that's the way Chris has always been."

A subtle, but important, change was taking place in McCarron as his career progressed and his family grew. He admits that in the beginning, he wasn't a horse lover. "The big thrill for me was the speed and getting your picture taken and having people give you high-fives, and looking at your check at the end of the week," said the rider. "Then my girls started riding show horses shortly after they could walk, and I began going to horse shows and visiting the barn and watching my kids treat a pony like it was their sister or brother.

"Now I'm a horse lover to the nth degree. The thrill for me today is all those other things, plus getting an uncooperative horse to cooperate with me. Especially a horse that doesn't cooperate with other riders, whether it be extreme nervousness, being fractious, stubborn, or flat out refusing to go. In watching the horse shows, I realized that the philosophy that succeeded was the spirit of cooperation, rather than telling a horse he's got to do something. You always ask first, and if that doesn't do it, then you work on building trust further before you resort to force. It's something that really fascinates me — how some people can get horses to cooperate with them. Two great examples are Pat Day and Bill Shoemaker. Shoe was absolutely incredible at getting lazy horses to run, and he was not an especially strong individual. It's intangible, that communication."

To illustrate that point, several of McCarron's biggest wins have taken place on horses he was riding for the first time. He piloted Go for Gin to Kentucky Derby roses at first asking, won the Preakness on Pine Bluff first out, the Belmont Stakes with Danzig Connection, and the Travers aboard Forty Niner. "Communication skills are more important in those first-time situations," McCarron observed. "It's not always a tremendous benefit for a rider to know a horse beforehand, as long as the horse is relatively straightforward and doesn't have bad habits that will complicate matters. Go for Gin, Pine Bluff, and Forty Niner were relatively straightforward. Danzig Connection had some quirks, and the communication becomes more important then.

"(Trainer) Woody Stephens told me before the Belmont that Danzig Connection didn't want to be messed with. He told me not to fight him no matter what, and don't move until you absolutely have to. Well, the horse relaxed well for me because I wasn't fighting him, and he responded very favorably when I asked him to run because I was very patient. I never hit him — I waved the stick at him the last sixteenth of a mile and he drew away."

Adversity interrupted McCarron's escalating career in October 1986, when he was involved in a nasty five-horse spill during the Oak Tree at Santa Anita meeting. Fifteen years later, looking out at the exact spot at the head of the stretch where it happened, McCarron recalled the mental recuperation was more difficult than the physical, which was testing enough. "People kept telling me, 'Boy, are you lucky.' I was lucky? I broke my leg in four places. But in the overall scheme of things, yeah, I guess I was. You ask yourself if you want to accept that risk again, and it's a pretty substantial barrier to break through for someone who has concern for his well-being and for being able to provide for his family as opposed to becoming a burden on the family.

"There is absolutely fear, and if anyone tells you they don't experience that, they've got nerves of steel and ice water running through their veins, and I think they're full of it. Injuries on the racetrack cause fear in riders. But fear can be an emotional mechanism from which we're able to exercise caution. I think the majority of us have the ability to put those memories in the back of our minds and suppress them so we can rise to the point where they don't inhibit or impair our ability to perform."

McCarron was off the track for six months, coming back to ride in mid-March 1987. He didn't really have time for the fear. Six weeks after returning, McCarron won the Kentucky Derby.

Ask fans about their most memorable Kentucky Derby of the past fifty years and the 1987 version likely outpaces any others. Alysheba stumbled and almost fell with sixteen horses breathing down his neck, a sure prescription for disaster. It brought McCarron his most exciting career moment.

"A perfect example of maintaining focus," McCarron said. "The split second of trying to prevent him from falling, trying to assist him getting back on his feet, reaction and reflexes took over, and the gravity of the situation never flashed through my mind. What a wreck that would have been, because everybody's got their head buried and driving at the three-sixteenths pole. Nobody's looking up, that's the narrow-minded focus. It hit me when I was on the podium with Jim McKay and trainer Jack Van Berg watching the replay: 'Oh God, the sixteen horses right behind me.' "

McCarron's skill and attitude are not lost on his clients. "The thing I truly love about Chris is he takes great care of your horse," said owner Trudy McCaffery, who along with John Toffan has put McCarron on horses such as champion Bien Bien and grade I winners Free House and Bienamado. "We had Kumari Continent in a stakes race, and Chris felt something was wrong and took her out of the race. Turns out she had a broken back leg. Had he ridden her out there might have been severe damage. There are jockeys, because it was a stake, who would have ridden her to the wire. Now she's in the breeding shed and she's healthy.

"If a horse isn't in the race, he'll look after it instead of getting into him. And the horse will come back and run better next time for him because there's a trust there."

In 1990 McCarron was involved in another bad spill, this one at Hollywood Park, resulting in two broken legs and a broken arm. Although he was off less than three months, perhaps there was some residual effect. The rider's win percentage dipped from the low twenties to between sixteen percent and eighteen percent from 1991 to 1995. During that time McCarron decided to switch gears and began riding fewer races, leaving the lower-level contests to others while he concentrated on allowances and stakes. Instead of riding from 1,000 to 1,500 races a year, McCarron scaled back to between six hundred and nine hundred. The reaction from fans and horsemen, by and large, tilted toward the negative.

"That was a tremendous challenge," conceded McCarron, "because trainers and owners want to ride extremely ambitious individuals who are competitive. And I am. But when I turned down mounts, trainers had difficulty understanding how I could say no and still be competitive. They figured 'he's got a lot of money and he's complacent.' And nobody wants a complacent rider. I overcame that through successful performance, showing them that when I'm out there to ride, I'm out there to ride, and ride hard. In order for me to maintain a level of ambition and prevent a sour attitude from setting in, I have to pace myself. Mentally and physically. And I think I've become a more effective rider."

Trainer Jenine Sahadi, who has paired McCarron with such standouts as The Deputy and Golden Ballet, said, "I don't see how anyone could question his commitment. There are not a lot of the big guys who are out there working horses every single morning. Chris is. And I won't question him if he decides to ride less races. He's very loyal, he's concerned about the horses he rides, and his work ethic is unbelievable.

"One other thing," said Sahadi, "is the way he treats my employees. He shows up a couple days after a stakes win with a check for the groom and the exercise rider. He knows them by name and treats them with the respect they deserve. He's involved with the help, and you can't say that about a lot of riders. And you can't buy stuff like that."

From those in the grandstand who don't know him came whispers in the nineties that McCarron would no longer take chances during races, that he wouldn't try to go through holes along the rail or between horses, that he wasn't capable of winning close contests. The rider heard it all. "That stuff would insult and offend me, but I've learned to ignore comments like that," he said. "All too often people come to opinions without knowing the facts. I'm guilty of the same thing. I'm way too quick to judge at times. And when I recognized that fault in me, I realized that fault lies in a lot of people."

Certainly the facts don't support the criticism. His win rate has been at or above twenty percent since 1996, with the exception of 1999, when it was nineteen percent. And as far as being able to finish, McCarron has won five Breeders' Cup Classics, none by more than half a length. That was the margin when Alysheba defeated Seeking the Gold in 1988. One year later, Sunday Silence turned back Easy Goer by a neck. McCarron and Alphabet Soup prevailed by a nose over Louis Quatorze and a head over Cigar in 1996. In 2000, Tiznow defeated Giant's Causeway in a stirring stretch drive. One year later, the McCarron and Tiznow team was at it again, coming back from what looked to be a sure loss to head another European, Sakhee, on the wire. Tiznow thus became the first horse to win two Breeders' Cup Classics. These victories don't happen by accident.

"When I rode Tiznow in the 2000 Goodwood, I hit him left-handed a couple of times and he got away from it. So in the Breeders' Cup I only hit him once and waved at him. I was fearful that because Giant's Causeway was so close to me, I didn't want Tiznow to bump him. I wanted to hit him, but I told myself 'Don't do it.' The thoughts go back and forth in milliseconds. And you can't worry about taking blame if he loses, because that's a loss of focus right there."

The stakes winners keep coming for McCarron, now in his mid-forties. In 2001 he won twenty-seven percent of the stakes races in which he rode. He passed the seven thousand mark in career wins early that year.

Off the track McCarron focuses on helping other jockeys. As a kid, Chris watched his father raise charity dollars for the Catholic Church via picnics. That commitment to service stayed with him. So when comedian Tim Conway

McCarron and Tiznow, back to back in the Classic.

suggested establishing a fund to help riders, Chris and Judy jumped in wholeheartedly and helped Conway start the Don MacBeth Memorial Jockey Fund, named for the talented jockey who died of cancer in 1987. Through fundraising events that McCarron works tirelessly on, the fund has helped 1,200 injured riders. McCarron helps raise about $250,000 annually for it.

"It's very satisfying to help less-fortunate riders, but very depressing at the same time," he said, "because I think this industry can do a whole lot more toward offering financial assistance to that end. I think charitable organizations should get a percentage of the handle. It's a sad state of affairs that several times a year I have to go to people and ask them to attend an event for injured jockeys, or injured horses, for that matter. It should be something that's automatic in this industry, considering what we contribute to this sport."

In addition, McCarron makes himself available to help market racing, be it through commentating on television when he's injured or doing interviews with the media. "I am an avid golfer and love golf, but I can't tell you how irritating it is for me that people think watching golf is more exciting than going to the races. Racing has failed to market us."

Citing a drop in his enthusiasm level, McCarron surprised the industry by announcing his retirement in June 2002. He went out a champion, winning the Affirmed Handicap aboard Came Home in his final trip around the oval. A large crowd turned out at Hollywood Park to witness the ceremonies that honored him. McCarron will likely continue to take an active role in improving the plight of jockeys and racing as a whole. This particular mind would be a terrible one for the industry to waste.

10

COREY NAKATANI

Nak Attack

One morning in the early 1990s, just a few years after he began his riding career in Southern California, Corey Nakatani was standing on the Hollywood Park backside, talking with a trainer. Christopher Speckert, a conditioner mostly known for champion older horse Pleasant Tap, came by. "Hey, Corey, can you come by and work one?" he asked. Most jocks would reply with a "I'll be right over" or "I'm already working one," the polite way of bowing out. Nakatani's reply? "I'm not gonna work your horse. In the afternoons you just put me on your shit ones anyway."

Welcome to the world of Corey Nakatani, a provocative mix featuring heaping portions of ability and attitude. Early in his riding career, Nakatani was infamous for telling trainers exactly what he thought of their mounts after a race. But it is his tremendous athletic ability, not his diplomacy, that draws trainers to the thirty-one-year-old. They talk about his seat on a horse, his strength, his confidence, and his patience with horses, characteristics that from the beginning belied his young age. Nakatani, for better or worse, came from origins that forced him to grow up quickly.

Nakatani is of Japanese-American ancestry. His grand-parents were interned during World War II at a camp in Colorado before being transferred to another in California. There they gave birth to Corey's father, Ray. As a baby, Ray lived in an internment camp in the Los Angeles area — a place called Santa Anita Park. That is just one of several ironies that pop up along the path of Corey Nakatani's career.

But it was not his ancestors' situation that motivated Corey to succeed in his chosen profession or instilled his aggressiveness. Instead, he points to a childhood in which he grew up one of ten children. "I had to fight for a pair of socks to wear to school," he remembered. "If you wanted a bowl of cereal before leaving the house, you had to jump in the shower early. I didn't grow up with any silver spoon in my mouth.

"My dad had a heart attack when I was ten (Ray Nakatani died in 1997). I went to work raking leaves and mowing lawns and selling Christmas trees to make money for my mom so we could pay the bills and feed the kids. After school I'd work in a restaurant peeling potatoes and making French fries just so we could get by. It all makes a big difference. And I wouldn't change that for the world. I've always been someone who worked hard, and my dad was the same way. You're not going to get anywhere in life if you don't. Either put your best foot forward or do nothing at all."

Nakatani channeled his early aggressiveness into wrestling, becoming an outstanding grappler at Northview High School in Covina, California. He liked the individual nature of the competition. "In wrestling it's you and nobody. You don't have a lot of backing — you've got to be strong and agile and have balance and athleticism. From there it's mental preparation and desire."

It was a wrestling mishap, in fact, that led to Nakatani's career as a jockey. He had broken a nose in a tournament and his father was giving him a ride home when the two stopped at Santa Anita. The track piqued Corey's interest, and he asked his father if jockeys made any money. His dad, a race fan, in turn asked trainers such as Jack Van Berg, and found out that indeed the top riders made a nice living.

"I was a good athlete — give me a baseball bat and I could hit," Nakatani said. "Give me a tennis racquet and I could do that. I had no fear, I was aggressive, and I was small. All I needed was a chance."

So the seventeen-year-old walked over to the barn of trainer Roger Stein in 1987, saying he wanted to work. It took Nakatani all of three days of mucking stalls and walking horses before he approached the trainer. "Hey boss man, put me on one of these horses," Nakatani said. Asked whether he'd ever ridden a horse before, Nakatani replied, "No, but I can do this."

"The thing that struck me," said Stein, "was that he was really that confident. He felt he could do what he was asking me. Not that I ever gave him a horse to gallop. This isn't a game here, and people can get hurt. He figured he could just walk on the racetrack and start galloping horses. And he probably thought he could gallop horses starting Thursday and ride races on Saturday."

Stein advised the youngster to go to a farm and gallop horses for a while, then come back to the track. Nakatani wasn't crazy about doing it that way, but he listened. He worked grooming horses at the farm of Tony Matos, who would become Nakatani's agent shortly afterward. Corey

169

then began breaking and galloping horses for riding legend Johnny Longden. He graduated from the jockey school in Castaic, California, just north of Los Angeles.

"I was very fortunate to learn the right way — by grooming them, taking care of them, getting on them, knowing the problems and how to fix them, and having a feel of how each horse traveled," Nakatani said in retrospect.

By 1988, at age eighteen, Nakatani was riding across the border in Caliente, Mexico. By the spring of 1989, he joined the tough jockey colony at Santa Anita.

"This kid is as good as Pincay and Cordero," Matos claimed of the twenty-year-old Nakatani. Some hyperbole by an agent touting his client? Maybe. But it should be remembered that Matos handled the books of Cordero and Pincay as well. "He has the patience of Delahoussaye, the strength of Laffit, and the brains of Shoemaker," Matos enthused. "Corey is a cold-blooded rider."

The early results back up Matos' claims. Nakatani was by far the leading apprentice on the Southern California circuit in 1989 and led the nation's bug boys with nearly $2.5 million in purses earned for the year. To kick start Nakatani's career as a journeyman, trainer Henry Moreno put him on a bunch of live mounts. D. Wayne Lukas legged him up on the sensational three-year-old filly of 1991, Lite Light. Nakatani piloted the daughter of Majestic Light to grade I scores in the Coaching Club American Oaks, the Santa Anita Oaks, and the Kentucky Oaks.

"Corey went and paid his dues and learned his craft," noted Stein. "In the thirty years I've followed horse racing, I can't think of anyone who learned any quicker than he did."

Nakatani married trainer Wally Dollase's daughter, Michelle, who runs a lay-up facility in Bradbury, California, called Overview Stables. The couple has three children. Early on, Corey received some help from his father-in-law, namely the mount on Itsallgreektome, who would win an Eclipse Award as champion grass horse in 1990.

"Corey has a great attitude," said Wally Dollase. "He's a winner at whatever he does, from riding to ping-pong. He's tenacious, and since he's my son-in-law, I was trying to help him out."

Victories on Lite Light brought Nakatani early renown.

The gray gelding Itsallgreektome won the Hollywood Derby and the Hollywood Turf Cup under Nakatani, yet was sent off at odds of 36-1 in the 1990 Breeders' Cup Mile at Belmont Park. It was Nakatani's first Breeders' Cup mount. "I was very high on the horse," he recalled. "He had a cocky attitude and was a tough horse to ride. Wally and Michelle spent a lot of time getting him right. He blossomed when we got him on the turf. I remember being in New York with Jimmy the Greek before the race, and he told me the horse had no chance. I told him I'd bet him horse for horse, but he wouldn't do it.

"I was sitting five lengths back, tracking them down on the hedge, then turning for home I moved out and made the lead. But I hit the front too soon for Belmont. He kicked clear of them, then went to goofing around, and the other horse (Royal Academy) ran him down. We got beat a neck."

That marked the start of several live Breeders' Cup longshots that Nakatani piloted to on-the-board finishes. In 1993 he brought the Argentine import Re Toss from far back at 18-1 to finish third, only two and a half lengths behind Hollywood Wildcat and Paseana. A year later in the Distaff, Nakatani rallied from eighth on 77-1 Miss Dominique to again finish third.

"Henry Moreno didn't know whether to go to the Breeders' Cup with Re Toss, and I remember telling him 'Let's take a shot. What have we got to lose?' She ran a big race in one of the better filly divisions in Breeders' Cup history. It's one of those situations where you go in with everything to gain. I love that. I don't get nervous. I've always wanted to be the one in control."

Nakatani found himself in the middle of one of the greatest Breeders' Cup contests to date — the 1994 Juvenile

Fillies, which showcased his mount, Serena's Song, and Flanders. The two classy fillies ran eight and a half furlongs in lockstep, never more than a head separating them. Nakatani and Serena's Song finished second by that head.

"One of the most thrilling races I've ever been part of," Nakatani said. "Serena's Song was giving it her all, and Flanders on the inside with Pat Day was giving it her all. Down to the wire they were head and head, but that last little bit we couldn't hold her off. I thought I had her every step of the way. It was just a step too far."

There was another, uglier, side to the suddenly escalating riding career of Nakatani. The aggressiveness and the attitude that combined to make him so competitive and successful cut against him at the same time. A series of suspensions and fines dogged him in the early nineties for things such as careless riding and misuse of the whip. He was fined in early 1995 for whipping a recalcitrant horse on the head during a post parade at Santa Anita. He was ruled off for three days in September of that year, and for another five days in December for interference disqualifications. Nakatani threatened to sue the stewards. "He'll have to get in line," said steward Pete Pedersen.

At the end of what should have been a landmark year for Nakatani, things turned particularly grim. Third behind only Jerry Bailey and Gary Stevens in purse earnings for the year, Nakatani on December 29, 1995, had the mount on Tillie's Joy, the favorite in a maiden-claiming event at Santa Anita. The two-year-old son of Native Prospector ended up sixth, and on the ride out, Nakatani used his whip to hit the horse. Moments later, Tillie's Joy was in distress, having fractured his left fore cannon bone. He had to be euthanized.

Under California Horse Racing Board rules, jockeys are prohibited from using the whip before or after races except to control the horse, which Nakatani maintained he was doing. They are also prohibited from hitting the horse on the head, which Nakatani was accused of doing. Videotape replays were not conclusive as to where the jockey struck the horse. Although the racing board ultimately found no link between the alleged whip misuse and Tillie's Joy's breakdown, the sport had been damaged. One local newscast teased its sports report by asking, "Did a jockey whip a horse to death?"

At the time, Nakatani already had seven whip violations on his record. He admitted using the whip to keep the colt straight while galloping out and said he was unaware that the horse had suffered an injury at that point. He was suspended five days and fined five hundred dollars for using the whip in an improper manner.

The tough times had only just begun. In October of 1996 Nakatani's sister Dawn was found strangled to death in the laundry room of her Baldwin Park, California, apartment. Dawn Nakatani had a two-year-old son. "It hit me pretty hard. I was in a daze," Corey said.

The incident occurred just one month before his finest day in the saddle, the 1996 Breeders' Cup at Woodbine, where he won a pair of races. He dedicated the two victories to Dawn.

"It was unbelievable, like I had an angel on my shoulder," the rider said of his afternoon. "It was a very special day. An unbelievable day. I had a lot of mixed emotions with my family and everything. You do something that not a lot of people can say they've done — something I worked so hard for. It was a day I'll never forget. Dawn does a lot of things for me. I just hope she is in a better place and that she is in peace now."

His first win that Breeders' Cup Day was aboard the brilliant sprinter Lit de Justice, a gray son of El Gran Senor who had a world of speed but also a bagful of antics. "He had a lot of character, and you had to do weird stuff with him," said Nakatani. "I used to work him the wrong way around the racetrack, turn him in circles, do stuff to keep him confused. Jenine (Sahadi, Lit de Justice's trainer) had faith in me and gave me free rein to work with the horse."

Sahadi had also told Nakatani to keep the horse on the outside during the previous year's Breeders' Cup Sprint at Belmont Park, and Nakatani felt that cost him the race at 14-1. "I could have gone down inside and cut the corner and won, but the horse had been stopped in his previous race, so they wanted to go around. It cost us the race, and I regretted riding him that way."

There were no mistakes for the encore at Woodbine. Nakatani sat with Lit de Justice down at the rail, then found a seam between horses and the late-charger showed his stuff, passing four horses in the final furlong to win by better than a length. "You make a mistake the first time, you don't let it happen again," the rider explained.

But he wasn't finished. In the Distaff, Nakatani partnered the brilliant filly Jewel Princess, aboard whom he had won the Vanity Handicap at Hollywood Park. Nakatani put the daughter of Key to the Mint in a stalking position and then fired down the stretch, ironically defeating Serena's Song for all the money. "I was sitting in the right spot and it opened like the Red Sea," said Nakatani. "She's the best filly I've ever ridden."

Shortly after the Breeders' Cup, Dawn Nakatani's former boyfriend was arrested for her murder, giving some relief to the Nakatani family. "We're not looking over our shoulders anymore," Corey said at the time. He took off to do some riding in Japan and returned to California for the Hollywood Park Turf Festival. After riding a poor race aboard Wandesta in the Yellow Ribbon Stakes at Santa Anita in October, Nakatani retained the mount for Bobby Frankel and Juddmonte Farms for the Matriarch at Hollywood. Wandesta and Nakatani defeated archrival Windsharp by a half-length for a measure of redemption.

Nakatani found himself aboard a barn full of stars during 1997. Jewel Princess was still in top form, winning the

Lit de Justice gave Nakatani his first Breeders' Cup win.

Santa Margarita and the Santa Maria handicaps. There was a new star in the Dollase stable — Sharp Cat, a brilliant filly whom Nakatani partnered to capture the Las Virgenes and the Santa Anita Oaks. Nakatani also had graded stakes wins in 1997 with Deputy Commander, Worldly Ways, Yashmak, and Sandpit. During the early part of the year, though, Nakatani's father died. Then, during the summer, an incident at Del Mar put Nakatani in the headlines again.

On August 3, Nakatani had Boldly Ruhl down at the rail in an allowance race when apprentice rider Ryan Barber began hitting the race favorite, Policy Maker, right-handed. Policy Maker lugged in, forcing Nakatani to take up sharply on his mount. As the horses were pulling up after the race, Nakatani and Barber fell in alongside one another and exchanged words. Nakatani then unleashed his forearm, hitting Barber on the shoulder and knocking the apprentice off his mount. Nakatani was suspended for the remainder of the Del Mar meeting and ordered by the stewards to get counseling for anger management. His license was put on probation for a year. Nakatani acknowledged making a mistake and accepted the ruling.

Given the benefit of several years' perspective, Nakatani was asked whether he felt more mature for all his experiences with suspensions. "I'm in the heat of battle out there. I'm a competitor and I want to win, and I do what I think is right at the time. My ass is on the line, and you've got people out there who shouldn't be out there affecting the outcome of races. When I got put through the rail at Hollywood Park, no one said a word. Nothing happened. If someone comes and spits in your eye, are you gonna let them do it?

177

"If somebody pulled a gun on you, are you gonna try and shoot them or let them shoot you first? I ain't gonna stand there and go, 'Oh, you gonna shoot me?' You have to look at things in reality. You don't know what you'd do until the situation happens. It's easy to sit here and say 'I wouldn't do this' or 'I wouldn't do that.' But I can't say I wouldn't do it again. I know one thing — I'm going to defend myself.

"I think racing's gotten lackadaisical in giving licenses to ride. You should have to go to school and qualify; then you should have to ride at a 'B' racetrack for a year. Make a stipulation that you have to ride fifty winners at a 'B' racetrack before you can move up. Then start your bug. But they do that as an apprenticeship at an 'A' racetrack instead. These aren't my decisions, but if they were I'd change that."

Whatever has gone on in Nakatani's life and in his head seems to have little effect on his performance. His win aboard Lit de Justice in the Breeders' Cup Sprint was the beginning of a three-year winning streak for the rider in that race. Sahadi once again gave him a leg up before Elmhurst came firing down the Hollywood Park stretch to capture the 1997 edition from far back — a perfectly judged ride that resulted in a then-record time for the race. In 1998 at Churchill Downs Nakatani went to the front of the Sprint field on Reraise and never looked back, winning the contest for his brother-in-law, trainer Craig Dollase.

"I guess I was in the right place at the right time," Nakatani said of his three Sprint triumphs. "Jenine had Elmhurst going so good. And Reraise, I felt like I never even got to the bottom of him. He felt so strong and just galloped along and never took a deep breath."

"Corey has such great patience and vision," said Craig Dollase. "He makes the right moves because he can see things unfold. And he's a competitor who fears nothing."

That notion was seconded by Roger Stein. "All the great riders go out there without any fear," he said. "Yet they're all faced with knowing what could happen. When most of them see a spill, they'll think 'that could have been me.' When Corey sees a spill, he says 'there's no way I could have been in that.' On top of his confidence and athletic ability, Corey is fearless."

Gradually, the negative headlines are fading as Nakatani continues to grind out winners. His eighty-two trips to the winner's circle at Santa Anita in the spring of 2000 brought him his second riding title for that meet. He also owns crowns from Hollywood Park (1995), Del Mar (1994), and Oak Tree at Santa Anita (1994-95). Although his Sprint streak was scissored when Regal Thunder finished up the track in 1999, Nakatani had his picture taken after the Breeders' Cup Mile aboard Silic.

"I got to figure out a few things about him," Nakatani said. "It's all about knowing your horse, getting him in the right situation, and letting him perform. Some horses will relax and some won't. You have to go by instinct. You can't sit there ahead of time and plan it out. When these horses are feeling strong and wanting to do things, you stay out of their way and let them do it.

"That's what I picked up from guys like Laffit Pincay and Chris McCarron. They're very patient on their horses. They let the horse dictate what it wants to do."

One horse who appeared to have no ceiling was Sharp Cat, who continued on with Nakatani in 1998 to win the Ruffian and the Beldame at Belmont Park and the Chula

Vista Handicap at Del Mar. Trained by Wally Dollase, she looked the part of the Breeders' Cup Distaff winner. However, one week before the race, she suffered a nervous condition called "tying up" and nearly lost her life. As it was, she was retired, and shortly thereafter The Thoroughbred Corp. fired Dollase as its private trainer. In yet another twist, Nakatani ended up riding Anees in the 2000 Kentucky Derby — for The Thoroughbred Corp.

So it goes in the career of Corey Nakatani — for each achievement there seems a bittersweet twist. He earns a good deal of his living at Santa Anita, where his grandparents and father were imprisoned. He rides his most successful Breeders' Cup a month after the murder of his sister. He rides in the world's biggest race for the people who fired his father-in-law.

"That's all in the past, and I don't look that way," Nakatani said. "I look forward. This is a business, and I don't think about what went on before. I go play golf."

Smacking the small ball around may be what finally gets the jockey to relax. After awhile, of course. "When I started playing, I didn't have patience. I had a lot of broken clubs. I thought I was Bo Jackson, breaking clubs over my knee. 'Wham.' But then I realized it wasn't the club."

Golf is also responsible for another Nakatani move — sticking his tongue out for the camera when he crosses the finish line first. It came out of playing with His Tongueness, Michael Jordan. "We started talking about the tongue thing," Corey said, "and I told him I was going to do it in a race. So I stuck it out after winning a big race at Santa Anita and Prince Ahmed Salman (The Thoroughbred Corp.) said I should do it more often, which was cool. So I do. Of course, then I get hammered for it in the press."

It just wouldn't be Corey Nakatani without the chip on his shoulder. His childhood battles for socks and cereal are never far away. You can see the intensity even in a loosely played game of cards in the middle of the jockeys' room at Hollywood Park. The other players are goofing around, getting distracted, talking across the room. Nakatani sits there, intense, keeping track of whose play it is.

He realizes that he's made mistakes, understands what it is to live with them, and tries now not to let them happen again. He's created a possible Hall of Fame career, a terrific achievement considering his somewhat late start in coming to the riding profession.

Has he mellowed? No. He's upset he didn't win the Eclipse Award for his stellar year in 1995, and he carries a grudge. He's upset with the politics of various bodies, including the Jockeys' Guild, which he resigned from in 1995. His comments on these and other topics have an edge.

Back in the beginning, when Nakatani was walking hots for Stein, the barn won a race at Los Alamitos. Said the trainer, "We have the picture in the winner's circle and Corey's in it carrying a bucket. Anytime he comes around here cocky we show it to him and remind him where he came from."

Nobody, except Nakatani himself, imagined how far the kid with the bucket would go.

11

LAFFIT PINCAY JR.

King Grand

L affit Pincay Jr.'s life has all the elements of a classic. He has fought decades of tough battles, raging
over obstacles both personal and professional. He's overcome tragedy and hardship to come back even stronger. To
get to the essence of his life, though, you need know only
a couple of things. First, when Pincay gets a leg up on his
mounts in the saddling ring at Santa Anita Park and heads
for the racetrack, he passes a bronze bust of himself.
Second, when he broke Bill Shoemaker's record in 1999 to
become the winningest rider of all time, every jockey at
Hollywood Park came running out into the winner's circle
with looks of joy, pride, and honor, as if each one of them
had accomplished the great achievement.

The other riders were not simply honoring a great
mark set by one of the most remarkable athletes of modern times, they were paying homage to a man in the truest
sense of that word. A man who did it the right way, who
rose above his self-proclaimed faults and twists in the road
that would have derailed mortals of less determination,
discipline, and perseverance.

Relegated to riding horses that could never match his

class or talent, Pincay was fitted for the rocking chair, slippers, and gold watch years before he became the winningest jockey. He had every opportunity to slip quietly into the long goodnight. He ended up raging against the dying of the light instead, and with the same will he's employed to carry so many horses across the finish line, so too he carried every naysayer who thought him too old, every fan, everyone associated with his sport, to heights of excitement and mass recognition scaled but a handful of times over many decades.

This man with the face etched in the classic features of the ancient ones who settled Central America, their ruins testament to the passing of the sands of time, pulled the entire industry of horse racing along on his back up the mountain. An industry that so often can't get out of its own way couldn't go wrong riding the powerful Pincay, honored by presidents and governments and everyone he ever touched in ways large and small.

Pincay, a fifty-two-year-old grandfather the day he broke Shoemaker's mark with his 8,834th win, is George Blanda kicking winning field goals for teammates half his age; Nolan Ryan into his mid-forties torching fastballs past hitters; Andre Agassi blowing passing shots past foes ten years his junior. To see Pincay in the jocks' room, muscles that he tries not to enhance bulging under his skin, it is impossible not to proclaim him the greatest athlete in the world. To see the respect accorded him by his fellow riders is to realize the dignity and sportsmanship and class he carries with him day in and day out. It wasn't always this way, but it has been long enough to celebrate the remarkable ride of Laffit Pincay Jr.

He was born December 29, 1946, in Panama City,

Panama, the son of a notable jockey who soon after the baby was born divorced Laffit's mother and moved to Venezuela. Father and son have seen each other only a handful of times since and have never been close. The boy grew up with his mother and stepfather, and displayed athleticism, particularly in baseball. His dream of becoming a big-league second baseman was short-circuited by his size, so he decided at age fifteen to go to the racetrack and try to follow in his father's footsteps. To do so, he cut a deal with his mother: racetrack in the morning, school in the afternoon.

Having not grown up with or around horses, the young man had to start with the basics. "The first thing I had to learn was not to be afraid of horses," he said. "I had a lot of fear at first, and the horses are more wild over there in Panama. They get scared very easily and try to throw you off. If they see a car go by, anything like that, they get spooked.

"Then galloping was difficult because over there we had to learn bareback, no saddle. And breezing them bareback, it's very, very difficult. Once I learned that, I started putting a saddle on the horses and that's when I started to create my own style. I watched other riders and did my own things to create a style."

At seventeen Pincay rode his first race, finishing last in a seven-horse field but enjoying the experience. He realized how hard a job it was because of the way his legs hurt, but overall liked the feeling of it. He remembers well his second mount. The date was May 19, 1964. "It was the last race at Presidente Remon racetrack and it was getting dark and I was on a big longshot named Huelen. I rode him well, we won, and I was so excited I didn't sleep the whole night."

In the United States, meanwhile, a Georgia native

named Fred Hooper had made a fortune in the construction business, and his good luck had continued when the first horse he owned, Hoop Jr., captured the 1945 Kentucky Derby. Hooper subsequently enjoyed considerable success importing contract jockeys from Panama, notably Braulio Baeza. Two years after his maiden win, and by now the best rider Panama had to offer, Pincay signed on with Hooper and arrived at Arlington Park on July 1, 1966, with little more than an obsessive desire to succeed. Before unpacking his bags, Pincay was in the winner's circle aboard Teacher's Art, the first of a multitude of winners over Pincay's three-year contract with Hooper and his trainer, Cotton Tinsley.

Pincay had more trouble adjusting to life off the racetrack than on it. He never asked other riders for any advice. He admired their seat "because I didn't look too good on horses when I came to this country, and I learned that from watching other riders. But I did most things on my own, and I believed in my style because I got a lot out of the horses — they really ran for me. So I just wanted to polish my style.

"Life was difficult because I was lonesome. Not speaking the language at all made it very difficult. I tried to learn by watching TV. I didn't make friends because I didn't know how to speak English, and on top of that I'm very shy and quiet. So it was hard at the beginning, and there were times when I thought about going back to Panama, but I knew if I did that I'd regret it, so I decided to stay here and handle it the best I could. The dream of making it here kept me going."

While at Arlington, Pincay met the legend with whom he would be inexorably linked. Bill Shoemaker, at thirty-four nearly twice Pincay's age and the owner of better than five thousand wins, could see the talent in the young Panamanian from the get-go. "You could see he had the natural ability," Shoemaker remembered. Although the two were rivals on the track for the next twenty years, their mutual admiration has never cracked, and each is often quoted as saying the other is the greatest rider he has ever seen.

Pincay, though, first had to overcome a hot temper and a wild streak going back to his rough riding days in Panama. He admits to being very aggressive in trying to win, in the process taking chances and collecting suspensions. "There was no field patrol over in Panama," Pincay said, "and you could get away with a lot of rough riding. It took me a few years here to adjust." Looking at the elder

HORSE HUELEN

Pincay's first win, on May 19, 1964.

statesman he's become, it's hard to imagine Pincay as the hotheaded youngster who fought his way through the jocks' room, but that's who he was back at the beginning, earning "the Pirate" as his nickname. A skull and cross-bones tattoo adorns one of his arms; the other boasts the name "Jeanine," his second wife.

As he became more comfortable in the United States and his temper calmed, Pincay became the ultimate strength rider. He was brute power to Shoemaker's touch and finesse. Coming down to the wire in a close race, the one man other riders don't want to discover next to them is Pincay. He seems to will his mounts forward to victory.

The contract with Hooper expired, but Pincay didn't miss a beat. Having moved his tack to the West Coast, he became the pre-eminent rider in the country by the early 1970s, virtually owning the Eclipse Award that decade. He won the inaugural Eclipse in 1971, and then won again in 1973 and '74, and yet again in '79. His win percentage began at twenty percent and went higher from there, not slipping noticeably until 1990, an incredible run for any rider. Pincay teamed with Hooper to win several stakes on three-time champion Susan's Girl. He won his first Santa Anita Derby in 1968 aboard Alley Fighter, then won it again in 1972 with Solar Salute and again a year later on Sham, who shortly thereafter would become famous as Secretariat's foil in the Triple Crown races. By 1975 Pincay had already been inducted into racing's Hall of Fame.

Pincay's first Santa Anita Handicap victory came with the brilliant South American Cougar II in 1973, and before the decade was out he repeated with Crystal Water in 1977 and with the greatest horse he ever rode, Affirmed, in 1979. While regular rider Steve Cauthen was serving a suspension, Pincay and Affirmed partnered for a Santa Anita Derby win in 1978 just before the son of Exclusive Native won the Triple Crown with Cauthen in the saddle. But in 1979, when Cauthen lost aboard Affirmed in two consecutive races, Pincay got the mount back. Pincay and Affirmed went on a grade I-winning tear. It started in February with the Strub Stakes and continued that year to include the Santa Anita Handicap, the Californian Stakes, Hollywood Gold Cup, Woodward Stakes, and Jockey Club Gold Cup. Pincay and Affirmed won the horse's final seven starts, assuring Affirmed of a third consecutive year as a champion and two straight as Horse of the Year. Pincay knew Affirmed was something special long before that, however.

"Laz Barrera shipped him west his two-year-old season for the Hollywood Juvenile. When I worked him, he was looking around, not leveling. I was asking him, but he wasn't doing much. When I got off, they said he went in :58 and change and I couldn't believe it. I knew right then. He won the Juvenile by seven and you know the rest."

Whereas Shoemaker was known for his feathery touch and magically being able to get horses to run for him, Pincay is nothing if not a study in strength. Race fans out West point to any number of occasions when they've witnessed Pincay pick a horse up by the reins and carry him across the wire. But the rider was paying a heavy price for all his strength. Throughout his career, Pincay has had to battle weight more than any other top rider of his generation(s). He must somehow keep his powerful body at 117 pounds, an unnaturally low weight for his thick, stocky build. Once while driving cross-country he ate normally and after five days found himself near 140 pounds.

"I've had to fight weight since I started," said Pincay. "I tried to do everything. I went in the sweatbox, I took diet pills, I took water pills. I heaved my food. I realized that wasn't for me and thank God I only did that for a little while, a year. At one time I was doing all those things together — I was flipping my dinners, going in the sweatbox, taking diuretics, and I was just a mess. I was weak.

"I was going home one day during the seventies, I had just won five races on the card, and I was feeling lousy, really down. I thought to myself, 'Why am I feeling this way?' I should have been happy, but I was killing myself. I was winning, but I wasn't having a good time. I was working too hard and reducing and dieting too much. It's no good to live that way. I didn't know how to get out of it, but I knew I had to do something."

As well as Pincay was riding, he felt he should have been doing even better. What he had in his corner was youth and that incredible desire to succeed. So he started learning little by little, jumping from one diet to another and trying to eat healthier foods. "I went to a nutritionist who helped me by giving me the basics of nutrition and telling me what was healthy to eat, telling me about protein and carbohydrates and things like that. So you can learn how to eat, but what they don't understand is the athlete has a completely different life than other people. You need to make your body give the best it can give. I had to learn that on my own, and I did. Nutrition to me is a science — you keep learning new things all the time."

The oldest saw in the racing game is you experience the highest of highs and the lowest of lows, and Pincay went on that roller coaster ride in the mid-1980s. After ten failed tries, he rode onto the track for the 110th running of the

Kentucky Derby aboard Swale in 1984. The Claiborne Farm homebred certainly had the credentials, being by Triple Crown winner Seattle Slew out of the Forli mare Tuerta. Conditioned by Woody Stephens, Swale was an outstanding five for seven as a two-year-old, and was second choice in the Derby behind the entry of Althea and

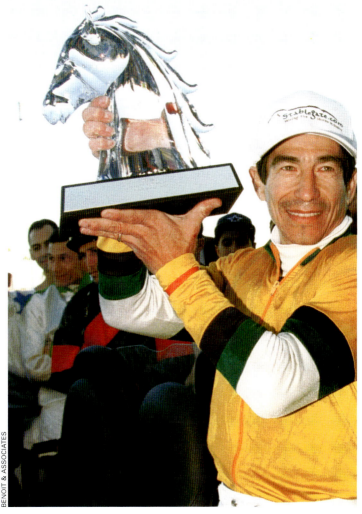

BENOIT & ASSOCIATES

After his 8,834th win, Pincay made the record books.

Life's Magic, a pair of fillies. Pincay knew Althea would set the early fractions and was quite confident she couldn't stay the course. So he got Swale away in good order and pressed the tempo.

After a mile, Swale assumed the front by two lengths, and Pincay went on with it to discourage potential threats. Opening up by five at the top of the stretch, they made it home by three and a quarter lengths over Coax Me Chad.

"That was a bigger thrill than anything that I experienced," Pincay said. "Bigger than the Hall of Fame. I knew about this race since I was a little kid in Panama. I remember Don Brumfield winning on Kauai King when I was just starting out, and that made a big impression on me because he said something to the effect that coming down the stretch God helped him to get there. You didn't just need ability or talent or luck, but help from above to win this race because you want it so bad.

"The rush of winning that race was unbelievable, maybe because for some riders it came easier — they win one and then they win another one. But for me it was very hard. I wanted to win it so badly, and after awhile I thought that maybe it wasn't meant for me. And then, boom, it caught me by surprise even though I thought my horse had a chance. When I saw I was going to win, when I passed that wire, the feeling was unbelievable. The emotion. It's something not too many riders are going to experience. Out of so many riders only a small bunch get to do it. That was a dream come true."

Swale and Pincay would add the Belmont Stakes to their portfolios that year, marking the third straight year Pincay and Stephens coupled to win the third jewel of the Triple Crown. Stephens was on his way to a spectacular five Belmonts in a row. As for the rider, who had won with Conquistador Cielo in 1982 and Caveat one year later, you have to go back to 1888 to find the last time someone rode three consecutive Belmont winners. That was before even Pincay's time. Yet Swale's triumphs in two legs of the Triple Crown were tempered by his sudden death after his Belmont victory.

Then in January of 1985, about six months after Swale's heroics, tragedy struck home. Pincay's wife, Linda, with whom he had two children, Lisa and Laffit III, was slow recovering from abdominal surgery. Infection and depression set in, and she felt she was becoming a drain on her

Pincay and Swale, the 1984 Derby winner.

family. "My wife was sick, depressed, I wasn't getting good mounts, everything was going the wrong way," Pincay remembered. One day Linda picked up a small-caliber handgun and killed herself in their Los Feliz home.

"After the suicide I thought about retiring, or at least not riding for a long time," he said. "Then I started thinking that 'I've got my two kids, I have my mother, I have to come out of this.' I got a hold of myself. I've only got this one life and I had seen so many people go down because of something that bothered them. I had been tough all my life, with my self-discipline. The best thing for me was to come back to riding. It helped me to forget. So two weeks later I began riding, and I had a good year that year. I wanted to forget, so I concentrated on my job and that made me have a good year. I actually won the Eclipse Award."

Two weeks after returning Pincay rode winner number six thousand, and shortly after that brought home number 6,033, moving past John Longden and behind only Shoemaker in career victories. Buoyed by an almost divine inspiration, Pincay enjoyed an extraordinary 1985. Skywalker won an emotional Santa Anita Derby for him. "My kids were there that day, and it was the biggest race I'd won since my wife died. It gives me chills every time I think about it." When Angel Cordero took off Kentucky Derby winner Spend a Buck, Pincay drove him home by a desperate head in the Jersey Derby, good for a $2.6 million bonus for winning those two contests. He steered Greinton to the Hollywood Gold Cup winner's circle and ended the year with a victory in the Breeders' Cup Juvenile with Tasso.

As the generation of Fred Hooper and Woody Stephens slowed down or passed from the racing scene and newcomers took over, Pincay, by the start of the 1990s, came to be viewed as past his prime. He entered the decade in his mid-forties, and his winning percentage dropped, regularly settling at between ten percent and fifteen percent. Many barns, with the notable exception of Bill Spawr, stopped riding him. He got to only three Kentucky Derbys in the decade, all with longshot also-rans.

All was not lost, however, as he remarried in 1992, to his current wife, Jeanine, giving him a better attitude and outlook, as well as another son, Jean-Laffit. Shortly after, daughter Lisa made him a grandfather. All that was left was to turn his career around, which wouldn't be easy considering the popular perception of him as clearly now in his twilight.

Anyone can be admired when he or she is on top. What singles out Pincay, however, is the pure class he displayed when his business went south. He never issued a complaint or an excuse. The quiet dignity with which he wins or loses was always in effect. If ever one led by example as opposed to words, it is Pincay. And that is why he earned the respect of everyone close or not so close to him. The joy that greeted his later accomplishments was proportional to the effort he had to expend getting himself off the canvas and back into the fight.

Performance-wise, Pincay throughout the mid-nineties was just another jockey in the deep Southern California colony. And with the horse population decreasing, mounts, let alone quality mounts, were increasingly difficult to come by. In 1997 Pincay managed just seventy-five victories and had mounts in just five graded stakes. He was still about 260 wins behind Shoemaker's magical 8,833, and although that chase was not the sole reason he continued riding — his love of riding for riding's sake has never been questioned — it seemed that if he wanted the record within a reasonable span of time, he would have to leave town for a lesser circuit, such as Northern California. He spoke of retirement, likely out of frustration, as by all accounts he was riding well, but small fields and age discrimination were taking their toll.

"I was very close to leaving," Pincay said of the Southern California circuit. "I didn't want to leave my family. We were already planning when my wife would visit me and when I'd come back home, and I was thinking that this going back and forth was going to be hard on everybody. Plus, I hate planes. So I figured I'd give it one more try. And I did. I decided to go to the gym more often, work hard, and change my diet, start eating things I never ate before."

The airplane never departed, and the rocking chair, well, Pincay actually does sit in it, but it is still in the jocks' room at Santa Anita, next to a tabletop upon which rest dozens of vitamin bottles. Pincay recommitted himself to improving his body, beginning an enhanced exercise program of walking, light weights so as not to build muscle, and the Stairmaster. Among the 850 calories he allows himself daily, he discovered fruit, "and that has made a tremendous difference in the way I think and feel. Your body and your brain need sugar. I never ate fruit before, and I saw the difference right away. It was unbelievable. I could do the crossword puzzle faster, retain more, ride better, everything. Unbelievable."

His 1998 win total went back over one hundred, leaving him one very good year away from Shoemaker. The way things had been going, 2000 seemed a likely target to break the record. That had a nice ring to it, being the first athlete to set a monumental mark in the new century. And that's the way it looked for all the world until the 1999 Oak Tree meeting in the fall at Santa Anita. Suddenly, the Pincay magic was back, and he was pulling winners out of his hat with increasing regularity. Needing thirty wins to catch Shoe, Pincay moved on to Hollywood Park for its thirty-one-day November/December meet. Pincay expressed his desire to get the record back at Santa Anita on his fifty-third birthday, December 29. But he couldn't wait that long.

Trainers looking for a piece of the glory began riding Pincay left and right. Bill Spawr, his biggest backer through the good years and lean, had had a falling out with Pincay's agent, Bob Meldahl, earlier in 1999, but now all was good again. Other trainers who rarely rode him were all over him. Nothing since the great Secretariat's 1973 campaign united the racing world quite like the coronation of Pincay, both because of the greatness of the impending accomplishment and the class of the man who took center stage.

Win number 8,833, the equalizer, came on December 9 at Hollywood Park for fellow Hall of Famer Jack Van Berg, known best as the trainer of Alysheba. The following day dawned under sunny skies and a powerful breeze, a perfect winter's day in Southern California. With each race the anticipation flowed — fans ready, the media and track officials on alert. But the trail went cold, and his first three mounts never threatened for the glory.

Then came the sixth event, a maiden special weight carded at one and one-sixteenth miles on the turf. Dick Mandella was sending out Irish Nip, a three-year-old bay colt by Irish River out of the Danzig mare Sugar Nipper, for the second race of his career. Because of the situation,

Mandella convinced rider Brice Blanc to give up his mount on him this day, and so it was Pincay wearing the colors of owners Ted and Martha Parfet of Hickory Corners, Michigan, who also bred the horse. The Parfets owned the Kalamazoo franchise of the International Hockey League, and they were about to be part of one giant goal.

Breaking from the inside post, Pincay ignored Mandella's pre-race instructions and put Irish Nip on even terms with Laps n'Bounds. Irish Nip sped across the turf and cornered beautifully. Up the length of the backstretch he and Laps n'Bounds raced as one into a fierce headwind. After putting that one away, Irish Nip appeared vulnerable to the late rush of Quiet One. But still under a hand ride, buoyed now by the strong tailwind and the powerful call of history, Irish Nip began widening as the grandstanders rose as one. Taking five backhanders from Pincay, Irish Nip crossed the wire two driving lengths in front, Pincay standing in the saddle and thrusting his magic wand aloft.

And then the sea of silks exploded from the jocks' room to surround the new king. Jeanine, his three children, and granddaughter joined him. And then his longtime rival and longer-time friend, Bill Shoemaker, arrived. "Shoe was the greatest rider I've ever seen, and that makes me very proud to have this record," Pincay told the crowd. And then he thanked his family, the track, the trainers who supported him, his agent, and "Mr. Fred Hooper, for giving me the opportunity to come to this country to ride for him." Soon after, he spoke by telephone to the 102-year-old Hooper.

Then there was the Porsche presented to him by the racetracks of Southern California, and a champagne shower from the jocks, who carried him to the scale to weigh out. And later on, a steak dinner. "It was four ounces, pretty big for me," Pincay said the following morning. "I chewed every piece fifty times." And then he was off to the track, "to see if I can win a couple of races."

He could, and finished as the leading jockey at the meeting at age fifty-two. At fifty-three, he took the 2000 Oak Tree title, and, during the course of it, passed nine thousand career wins. To show that wasn't a fluke, he won the Hollywood Park fall title (in a tie with Victor Espinoza), the 2001 main Santa Anita meeting, the 2001 spring/summer Hollywood Park meeting, and the 2001 Oak Tree title. Absolutely amazing. It is widely believed Pincay will take a run at 10,000 before calling it a day. And why not? He is still enjoying riding, he is getting better horses, his home life is fun, and his temperament couldn't be better.

"Sometimes my wife will ask me about something and say, 'Doesn't that bother you?' And I say, 'Listen, it bothers me, but I'm not going to let it bother me.'"

When other jockeys, particularly older ones, talk about their careers, they mention other riders who have accomplished this or that in their later years. Then they come to Pincay and can't even use the comparison to make their case. "He's from another planet," said Chris McCarron. "An anomaly," Jerry Bailey said. "The ultimate race-rider," noted Eddie Delahoussaye. "They don't make words to describe what he's brought to the game," said Pat Day. All of the above are Hall of Famers.

When John Longden surrendered the career win record to Shoemaker in 1970, he joined Shoe in a ceremony to mark the event. "I think it took a good man to set this record," Longden stated. "And a damn good man to break it."

You can say that again.

12

MIKE SMITH

Trouble —
When the UFO Is You

M ike Smith would no doubt agree that it's better to have scaled the pinnacle of his profession and come sliding back down than never to have excelled at all. But having reached the summit as a rider only makes it harder for Smith to regroup and try for the top once again.

Smith is a native of Roswell, New Mexico, the UFO capital of the country, and for the past three years, he must feel like he's been living in "The Twilight Zone." The spirit of Rod Serling paid a visit to Smith one August day in 1998 at Saratoga, forty-eight hours after he had won the Travers Stakes aboard Coronado's Quest.

Things were shaking out Smith's way. He possessed a healthy lead in the jockeys' standings, had outstanding mounts like Jersey Girl going well, and seemed for all the world as if he were ready to recapture the top spot of the riding world that he'd so magnificently leased in 1993 and 1994, when he won back-to-back Eclipse Awards.

Then came the ninth race August 31, a Sunday, the last day of the riding week. Looking forward to two days off, and aboard a nice big mare, all Smith was thinking about was getting around there, having his horse run well, and enjoying the

grand life in a beautiful setting. That all changed with a chain-reaction accident entering the first turn. Smith was thrown into the air when he and his mount, Dacron, were forced into the hedge. Rider Edwin Cotto was suspended thirty days for causing the accident. Meanwhile, Smith found himself suspended in the brush with two fractured vertebrae.

"One minute you're on top of the world; the next minute you're on your back," he said the following day while wrapped inside a body cast painted in the black-and-cherry colors of the Phipps family racing silks, which Smith had worn aboard standout Thoroughbreds such as Inside Information and Heavenly Prize. And then with the energy that makes Smith so appreciated, he found the silver lining and a smile: "I thank the Lord I didn't sever my spinal cord. I'd judge myself a ten for the fall, but a zero for the landing." Vowing to be back as soon as possible, Smith got up from his wheelchair and walked a short distance to the car that would take him home.

He is still waiting for the vehicle that will bring him all the way back professionally.

When a jockey slumps following a major injury, the gambling public and horsemen, with hearts of tin and memories shorter than a nose-at-the-wire, proclaim that the jock is riding scared. He won't go through holes. He's afraid to try his luck down at the rail. He just doesn't have the hunger anymore, the will to get the job done. The rider, for his part, understands where that opinion is coming from, but denies all of the above. He's not riding any differently; he's just not getting the same kind of mounts. Business doesn't just pick up where it left off months earlier. Just give me the "A" stock, he says, and I'll show everybody I can still do it.

Mike Smith, born in 1965, showed everybody he could

do it at an early age. He always knew he wanted to be a rider, from the time his family gave him a leg up at age three or four, so early he doesn't even remember. His father, George Smith, was a jockey, and Thomas Vallejos, his uncle, taught Mike how to ride. At the tender age of eleven, Mike Smith rode Quarter Horses around New Mexico's bush circuit. He left home at fourteen, dropping out of school to gallop horses at racetracks throughout the Southwest, and two years later scored his first Thoroughbred win at Santa Fe Downs.

"I was always pretty gifted as a horse person — knowing what a horse likes and dislikes," Smith noted. "Knowing how to handle a horse came to me at a very young age. I had to learn how to ride in a race. Everything in New Mexico was speed, speed, speed. When you get to the bigger leagues, you have to learn that patience plays a big part in this game. Pace, being patient, and different little tactics come to you as you watch the better riders."

After serving his apprenticeship at Sunland Park in El Paso, Smith decided to strike out for bigger pastures, but not on his own. "I was scared, and I wasn't leaving town unless my grandparents came with me," he said. Smith's grandfather owned a bar near Sunland Park and was about to retire anyway. He sold the business, and he and his wife bought a house in Hot Springs, Arkansas, near Oaklawn Park when Smith moved his tack there. They also traveled with Mike to Nebraska when he rode at Ak-Sar-Ben. "They stayed with me until they passed away. They were my main support," Smith said.

"Mike was young and had never been away from home," remembered his aunt, Elizabeth Brockmann. "He was a special kid, and Dad wanted to be there and do that for him. Mike was always polite, well mannered, and has a lot of charisma. I don't think he ever had any interest in doing anything else. He always wanted to ride horses."

Smith moved from El Paso to Oaklawn, Ak-Sar-Ben, Hawthorne, Canterbury Downs, and Churchill Downs. At Oaklawn he began learning some "little tactics" by watching Pat Day, Larry Snyder, and John Lively. He married Lively's daughter, Patrice. He met up with trainer Shug McGaughey at Oaklawn and rode Pine Circle to a sixth-place finish for the trainer in the 1984 Kentucky Derby, Smith's first. As the eighties drew to a close, Smith's fear of leaving the Southwest was a distant memory, and he decided to try New York.

"I took to New York really well. It never bothered me," he said. "People were surprised because some of my friends who tried New York didn't take to it. But to this day I love New York. It's such a great city, and there's so much to do, or you can live out in the country."

There was a new colony of jockeys to learn from, and Smith kept his eyes open, studying Angel Cordero, Jorge Velasquez, Jose Santos, and Jerry Bailey. "Riding there was a whole lot more aggressive. Just because you're on the best horse doesn't mean you're just gonna get to gallop around there. They made you work for it. You're talking top, top riders, and if you're gonna beat them, you're gonna have to earn it. That polishes you."

Hall of Fame trainer Allen Jerkens remembers that Smith succeeded right from the start. "Mike attracted a lot of attention because he was winning on horses that, if you looked at their past performances, were the second or third best in the race," Jerkens said. "He worked hard, and I think he's as good as anybody."

Smith's congenial personality also went a long way in advancing his career.

He is liked by virtually everyone who has come in contact with him. McGaughey calls him "a great guy," and when both lived in New York, they'd eat at one another's homes and go out together. Jerkens noted, "He's an awfully nice person, always been nice to the workers and the fans, and he doesn't get surly when things aren't going well."

Smith hit the charts aboard Thirty Six Red, who won the 1990 Wood Memorial, a $500,000 grade I race that was

Smith and Prairie Bayou, the 1993 Preakness winner.

the first big victory for the rider. He also partnered with 1991 older female champion Queena, and in 1992 rode Lure to victory in the Breeders' Cup Mile. The classy son of Danzig was dismissed as third choice at 5-1 that day at Gulfstream Park in what is usually among the most competitive of Breeders' Cup heats. Smith, however, hustled Lure to the front, rattled off quick fractions, and was never troubled. Lure became the first wire-to-wire winner of the Mile, besting Paradise Creek by three lengths in the end.

The following year at Santa Anita the team made it two Miles in a row. Lure, no longer a secret, was sent off the favorite, but also sent off from post twelve with a short run to the first turn. Forced wide into that turn, it took Lure and Smith a half-mile to gain the lead, but once they did, it was "déjà vu all over again," with Lure crushing his field under a hand ride. Lure presented Smith with the first two of his eight Breeders' Cup victories to date and put an exclamation point on a dream year for the jockey.

Smith was astride the 1993 Kentucky Derby favorite, the Loblolly Stable homebred Prairie Bayou, and finished second to Sea Hero that day. But as the Preakness approached, the signs couldn't have looked more positive. Smith was winning everything in sight. On Black-Eyed Susan day, he and Lure took the Early Times Dixie Handicap. He then won the main event with Aztec Hill.

Nothing for seven in Triple Crown mounts till that Preakness, Smith and Prairie Bayou had a troubled trip around the Pimlico oval. Reserved near the back of the field early, Smith still had to steady his horse when Union City broke down in front of him. (Ironically, Prairie Bayou would suffer a fatal breakdown three weeks later in the Belmont Stakes.) Smith had to angle out four-wide to find room on the second turn. Then Prairie Bayou ducked in coming down the stretch and was all out to best Cherokee Run, a horse Smith would ride to victory in the Breeders' Cup Sprint the following year, by a half-length. "I just tried to sit up there and look pretty," Smith said jokingly, downplaying the Preakness ride he laid down.

Still two birthdays shy of thirty, Smith had a year in 1993 that others only dream about. Lure and Prairie Bayou led the parade of horses on whom Smith won sixty-two stakes that year, smashing Pat Day's record. His mounts won at a 21.3 percent clip, finished second another 27.8 percent of the time, and earned a total of $14,024,815. Sky Beauty took four grade I stakes under Smith in New York, including a sweep of the Triple Tiara series.

"In my opinion, Sky Beauty would have lost two of those big races, the Alabama and the Oaks, if Mike Smith hadn't been riding her," said trainer Jerkens. "She was tailing off before the Alabama, and I didn't even want to run her. She wasn't eating so well, but right before the race she started to pick it up. In that race she was further off the pace than she liked to be and Mike nursed her along and made the lead at just the right time. It was one of my biggest thrills in the game," said a man who has had plenty of them.

For his riding efforts in 1993, Mike Smith won an Eclipse Award. "It was amazing," Smith said, thinking back to that magical time. "I was riding really powerful horses, great horses, and I was at the top of my game. But when you're riding the quality I was riding, it makes the game awful easy. I suppose that Preakness weekend was the crowning point of my career, but I didn't feel that way at the time. I was always having fun wherever I was, be it in El Paso at Sunland Park or winning big races. But the experience, the thrill of winning the big ones, it's not something you can describe or hand down to anybody. You have to be involved to understand the elation. Nothing else in life is quite like it."

If 1993 was amazing, 1994 was a worthy encore. Smith's record of sixty-two stakes wins lasted exactly one year, as he moved the benchmark up to sixty-six in 1994. His mounts earned $15,979,820. Not only was he the regular rider for champion older female Sky Beauty, but also picked up the mount on a wide-chested gray runner named Holy Bull. The eventual Horse of the Year would win eight times from ten starts as a three-year-old in 1994.

"What a horse," said Smith, still stunned by the talent of the Great Above colt years later. "Just a dream. The thing with him was to do as little as possible and stay out of his way, and that's hard to do sometimes, believe it or not. Any movement you gave him — you could wiggle your toe — and he'd respond to it. That's how good he was."

Coming off a Blue Grass Stakes win, Holy Bull threw in a clinker in the Kentucky Derby. "Not to take anything away from the rest of them, but he was much the best," Smith said. "For whatever reason it wasn't meant to be that day. He wasn't there; he wasn't the Holy Bull that I'd ridden every time before that and after that. He was usually such a showoff in the post parade, so full of himself. He just wasn't there. That was a hard, disappointing day, man, and I don't know what it was."

Holy Bull snapped back to win the Metropolitan Handicap, the Dwyer Stakes, the Haskell, and the Travers. Then came the Woodward in September at Belmont Park, against a field that included Derby winner Go for Gin and other grade I winners Devil His Due,

Disconsolate after Holy Bull's poor Derby performance.

Tinners Way, Colonial Affair, Pistols and Roses, and champion Bertrando. The three-year-old Holy Bull sprinted away from them to win by five lengths. "This was more than perfection," Smith said that day. "People saw something they've never seen before. Today I saw something I'll never see again."

Asked to explain those remarks, Smith, looking back, said, "When he made that massive move in the Woodward, I thought he grew wings. I never felt his feet hit the ground. We hit Mach One and Mach Two. He beat the best older horses in the country like they were nothing, and I didn't so much as touch him. There was probably another gear there. It's just amazing when a horse gets so right, and he was."

Holy Bull wasn't nominated to the Breeders' Cup and didn't run again until the following year at Gulfstream. The four-year-old, with Smith aboard, captured a minor stakes as a prep for the big event, the $300,000 Donn Handicap. In the Donn, he was sent off at 3-10, and around the first turn he was on the flank of the pacesetter, a horse named Cigar. Smith said he was coasting along while Jerry Bailey was pushing on Cigar as they hit the backstretch. There, Holy Bull took a bad step, the last step he'd take in anger on a racetrack. Cigar went on to win the contest, quietly tallying the fourth victory of his eventual sixteen-race win streak. Holy Bull was retired.

"To this day I think about what that rivalry would have been like," said Smith. "It's hard to compare them. When I rode Cigar early in his career, he wasn't the same horse — he had ulcers and he was hurting. I'm sure Jerry and I both are confident we'd have won the Donn, but that's the way it goes."

At about the same time, Smith collected his second consecutive Eclipse Award, and the hits kept coming. On a rainy Breeders' Cup card at Belmont Park in 1995, Smith posted a double with Unbridled's Song in the Juvenile and Inside Information in the Distaff. Unbridled's Song prevailed by a neck after being steadied on the turn. Smith paid him the ultimate compliment when he noted that he used to call the horse "a little Holy Bull. Nobody got to see how good he was because he had foot problems and ulcers, but he would have been a special kind, very talented."

Everyone got to see how good Inside Information was. She romped home by thirteen and a half lengths over a field that included Serena's Song, Lakeway, and Heavenly Prize. As Smith returned to the winner's circle, the rain let up and a gorgeous rainbow arched across the sky behind him. "That was pretty cool, wasn't it?" Smith laughed. "I had the cake and the icing that day. Believe me, she toyed with them, she never even ran. They could have wheeled her right back into the Classic."

In 1997 at Woodbine, not only did Smith win the Queen's Plate, he did so in front of the queen herself. Seeing both Awesome Again and Queen Elizabeth II for the first time, Smith had himself a highlight day. As the queen stopped by the paddock to greet each owner, Awesome Again let out several bucks to introduce himself, then carried the day over Cryptocloser. In the winner's circle Smith remembers it being quite an honor. "The queen said to me, 'Beautiful horse. I think a lot of him.' She loved Awesome Again; she really did. And looking at what he turned out to be (Breeders' Cup Classic winner), the queen has an eye for a horse, I'll tell you that."

Smith got another fine first-time result on a horse when trainer Sonny Hine named him aboard another big gray machine, Skip Away, for the 1997 Breeders' Cup Classic at Hollywood Park. The horse had been the career horse of jockey Shane Sellers, who happened to be Smith's closest friend. But after a second in the Woodward, Hine fired Sellers for Bailey, who subsequently got off Skip Away despite winning the Jockey Club Gold Cup with him. Smith and Skip Away won the Classic for fun, but Smith felt seriously conflicted.

"I rode him for me and Shane," he said. "I feel badly he wasn't on the horse, because the outcome would have been the same. We met at Oaklawn Park in 1983, just two young guys happy to ride in any race. We used to talk about what it would be like to ride in a race like this."

Smith was asked to compare the two gray streaks. "Skip Away was powerful and strong and he was a stayer, a lot of stamina. He could hit his best stride early and keep it going. Horses would get drunk trying to keep up with him. He'd continue on, and they'd be wobbling by the time they got to the quarter pole. He didn't have the gears Holy Bull did, he was more of a grinder, but oooh, if you let him hit that big stride early…"

Smith was the only rider who could unlock the mystery that was Coronado's Quest, a talented colt who was his own worst enemy. His pre-race antics included bucking, freezing, rearing up, and throwing riders. "Mike had a great knack with him," said trainer Shug McGaughey. "I'm not sure what it was, but he was a better horse when Mike rode him. Mike got him to win a grade I going a mile and a quarter, which was stretching the horse's limits. He had a great feeling for him, and it really hurt all of us when Mike got hurt."

As the calendar clicked over to 1998, Smith's decade-long run to prominence hit a roadblock. In March he was involved in a spill at Gulfstream, leading to what he thought was a common rider's ailment, a broken collarbone. Turned out he wasn't so lucky, having broken his shoulder in three places. He got well in time to regain his form, get back on a roll, and then go down again that horrific day at Saratoga.

Most of us can only imagine how difficult it would be to come back from an injury that serious. Not only must riders come back, though, they must answer the charge that they're not the same performer they were before the fact. Smith mulls that thought over. "Well, I came back too soon in 1999," he admitted, "because I wanted to ride in the Derby, and I got a chance to with Cat Thief, and we almost pulled it off (finishing third, beaten less than a length). After that race I should have taken off for another month and let it heal more. I was hurting a lot, and maybe that showed at times.

"I was banking on getting the same kind of horses back. If I had, maybe I could have gotten back on a roll again and people would have forgotten I'd even been hurt. But I didn't get the horses and didn't get on the roll. And that's when people really start talking."

Jerkens said he was sorry he didn't have better horses to put Smith on. "After an injury, if it so happens a rider has to go wide a couple of times, everybody starts saying they're scared to go inside," Jerkens said. "I never thought that about Mike. Things just don't go right sometimes. It was no fault of his own, just one of the things that happen in this game."

Added McGaughey, "When you're out for a while, a lot of the horses have gone to other riders. It's a competitive world out there. I tried to ease Mike back where I could, but you can't necessarily take other riders off because he'd ridden for you before. You have to bide your time and get the mounts back through the process. Mike just got into a rut."

As Smith continued to have trouble getting live mounts, the rut deepened. Breeders' Cup Day 1999 was a low point. In September, Smith had been the regular rider on Artax, Soaring Softly, and Cat Thief. All three won Breeders' Cup races two months later. The only problem was, Smith was watching them on TV, still struggling to get over his back injury, not only physically, but also mentally. Smith calls that the greatest adversity he has faced in his professional life. And for nearly three years since he has struggled to regain quality mounts.

"It will put a sour taste in your mouth. I was spoiled and I didn't even know it. Throughout my career I've made the most of my opportunities, and it was working great. It's always been a blast, but now, for the first time in my career, it's turned into being a bit of work, and we're going to see how tough I am. It's up to me to see if I can pull it off, if I can fight back."

Most people in racing maintain that there are a dozen or maybe two dozen top riders around the country who will get the job done given the right horse, and that little separates one from the next. But in a game where an inch can mean so much, the difference often comes down to confidence. Riders themselves constantly bring up confidence as the determining factor between when they're riding well and when they're just a little off their game. All admit to going through ups and downs each year, but more than anything, getting on a little roll and gaining confidence is key.

"When you have more confidence than the other guy, you make the right decisions," said Smith. "There are a million things going on during a race, and they add up. When you get a good horse and get on a roll, you'll make all the right decisions. It's like when Michael Jordan talked about 'being in that zone' where the bucket looked so big he couldn't miss. Same thing with riding. You'll wait longer than the other guy. Find the right hole. When you're going good you feel like you can get on the outrider's pony and beat 'em. That's the feeling you get inside you."

Hoping to change things around, Smith decided midway through 2001 to leave New York and head back West, to California. A couple of regulars in that colony, notably Kent Desormeaux, who went to Japan in an effort to spend more time with his family and less time riding, had temporarily left town. The move to California, it should be noted, has not proven out for several riders in recent years. "Jersey" Joe Bravo took a shot in 2000 and was back East in a matter of months. Japanese star Yutaka Take tried to make a go of the Golden State, but never made an impact. Short fields in California exacerbate the problem of breaking into a quality-laden colony.

"Hey, short fields are good if you're riding the right horse in them," Smith laughed. "Hopefully my name will mean something, not that I'm saying I'm huge or anything. But I've had my share of success, and I've done well out there. I've got to find the people to ride for. Sometimes change is good. I'm just seeing if I can spark something. Hopefully people will give me a shot. I can always come back to New York and pick up and work harder, but I'm gonna go try this. It's good to get away. Maybe you'll be missed a little and when you come back you're like a fresh face again.

"The top guys are still riding me; I'm just not riding

215

their 'A' horses right now. Right now the ball's in somebody else's court and they're rolling with it. It's just a matter of keep playing and keep playing and keep playing until I get the ball back. I'm not riding any differently than I have before, but I'd like to get that confidence level back that only good horses can bring you. I'm riding as confidently as I can ride for what I'm riding. I'm a firm believer that when it's your time, it's your time. I've been doing this all my life so I know. Fear of riding is not a problem. The only fear I have is not doing well again."

After a slow start in California, Smith came on strongly in the second half of 2001. He hit at a twelve percent clip for the year, and collected five graded stakes wins. He rode a very promising two-year-old filly, Ayanna, to victory in the Moccasin Stakes at Hollywood Park in mid-November. Smith has broken into quality barns, riding for trainers such as Neil Drysdale, Richard Mandella, and D. Wayne Lukas. In fact, he spanned 2001 and 2002 in style, winning the Monrovia Handicap on December 31 aboard Paga for Mandella, then coming back January 1 and taking the El Conejo Handicap on Snow Ridge for Lukas. In 2002 he has been aboard Azeri, who in mid-year was widely perceived as the best distaffer in training.

These victories would seem like good omens as Smith plugs away, waiting for the one top horse that will turn the tables and the perceptions. He is not bitter when he discusses the downturn in his business. No malice toward trainers who used to ride him but are now using other jockeys for their top stock. One positive result from the serious injuries is Smith's new fanaticism about working out and staying fit. He's become a gym rat while most of his peers are out hitting a golf ball around.

run the Nedra Matteucci (formerly Fenn) Galleries in Santa Fe. "If I had invested in art when my aunts told me to I wouldn't have to worry about anything," he laughed.

After thirteen years, he and Patrice are getting a divorce, although that is unrelated to his struggles on the track. "We just grew in different ways, and it's been a long time coming," he noted, "but we're the best of friends and we get along great. She's a wonderful person."

His "comeback," though, is always on his mind. "I'd be lying if I said it wasn't affecting my life. Athletes always say they leave the game on the field and don't take it home with them. Wrong. To be the best, it's on your mind night and day, no matter what anybody says. I eat, drink, and sleep it until I get it back. That's me. I'm healthy and determined now, and it's all heading the right way."

Need to Succeed

O ne of the most exciting and anxiety-ridden moments in racing occurs minutes before the Kentucky Derby on the Churchill Downs backstretch, where each entrant is paraded in circles before making the walk over the hallowed racing strip to the saddling paddock.

You can feel the heat coming off the trainers and owners, who are hoping they've thought of every possible detail, fretting they haven't, and trying hard to suppress the nerves that go along with being eligible to secure a permanent place in racing lore.

What you don't expect to see is a forlorn look such as the one worn by the man with the crystal blue eyes before the running of the 2000 Derby. That day he stared straight down into the Churchill dirt, boring through it as if he might rekindle memories, revive a passion by stirring up the particles of clay and sand. No, forlorn has no place here, especially for the assistant trainer of the talented colt Anees, who the previous fall captured the Breeders' Cup Juvenile at Gulfstream Park. In fact, this man rode Anees that day in Florida.

Perhaps, as he prepared for the start of the 2000 Derby,

he was remembering riding his three Kentucky Derby winners over the dirt into which he gazed. Perhaps he was remembering the glory and the blankets of roses and the triumphs. Gary Stevens at that moment seemed as out of place in his tie and jacket as a five-thousand-dollar claimer would be entering the starting gate of the Derby.

Stevens is as well-spoken a man as you'll find on the racetrack. He's intelligent and possessed of an intensity that is his best friend on horseback and his enemy at other times. For years, too many years, he rode horses and gritted his teeth through the pain of bad knees. The piper finally caught up with Stevens on December 26, 1999, the vaunted opening day of the California racing season, always a time fresh with promise. After a grinding ride in the Malibu Stakes at his home base of Santa Anita, Stevens bid race-riding an emotional goodbye.

"I found myself thinking about the pain instead of the horse I was on, and that's not being fair to the fans or the horsemen or the other riders," he said that day. "I was hoping for a Christmas miracle, but the pain wouldn't go away." And then a few days later: "I hope I'm not stupid enough to attempt to come back. I think I'm wiser than that."

But it was not stupidity, despite his strong words to the contrary, and Mickey Mantle-like knees that brought Stevens back to race-ride again after only nine months away. It was that intensity, the fire still burning inside, and his not knowing how to fulfill the hunger. While riding, he could use the adrenaline, allow it to flow through his five-foot-three body and let it drive him home ahead of the field. As a jockey he was able to convert his nerves and the pressure into positive energy. As an assistant trainer he didn't have that outlet, and it was eating away at him worse than the arthritis in his knees.

No, it was not out of stupidity that Gary Stevens returned to riding, triumphantly at that. It was because of who he is and what he learned during the first years of his life.

Stevens was the youngest of three sons (foal of 1963) born to Ron and Barbara Stevens. Ron trained Quarter Horses and Thoroughbreds in Caldwell, Idaho. He instilled the competitive spirit in his sons, who were involved in sports from an early age. Gary wanted to be a football player, but never grew big enough to make that a reality. He'd had a riding horse since the tender age of three, however.

"Horses were part of our life," he recalled. "They were always there, right outside the house. We'd walk to the garage, grab a bridle and a saddle, and go for a ride. Instead of riding bicycles, we rode horses. But I never cared about them until I galloped my first racehorse. My brother Scott had started to ride professionally, and I saw the money he was making and the enjoyment he was getting out of it, and I figured I'd like to try that. He talked my dad into letting me get up on a racehorse. That was it. I was hooked. The power was incredible. At age twelve I knew that's what I wanted to do."

It wasn't that straight of a line, however. At age seven Stevens had been diagnosed with Perthes syndrome, a disease that debilitates the hip socket joint. His right leg was sheathed in a metal brace for a year and a half, and his ability to walk without pain, let alone compete athletically, was in doubt. Yet in school he became a star wrestler, which earned him numerous scholarship offers from colleges. More schooling was not at the top of his agenda, however, and with his parents' consent, he left both school and home at sixteen.

He accepted an offer to apprentice for Southern California trainer Chuck Taliaferro, who had a knack for developing young riders, having given Steve Cauthen and Cash Asmussen their starts. Stevens spent less than four months in Los Angeles that time around, "but they were the best months of my career because it built my foundation style-wise. I saw those guys down there ride and saw who I had to emulate. I got the experience of working with top horses and top horsemen, and riding with the best jockeys in the world."

Gary Stevens won just four races in ninety mounts during that time, but like a minor league ballplayer who gets a taste of the big time, what he gained didn't show up in the numbers. "I tried to pick the three best guys I saw and combine their styles into one," Stevens said. "Those three were Bill Shoemaker, Laffit Pincay Jr., and Darrel McHargue. Laffit for his strength, Shoe for his hands and finesse, and McHargue for the way he looked on a horse. He had an unbelievable seat."

Stevens returned to Idaho with the experience tucked away under his silks and rode ten or twelve races a day in Boise, practicing the lessons he'd learned down south. As the eighties began, his name started popping up on stakes winners at Yakima, Portland Meadows, and Longacres. In 1985, aged twenty-two, Stevens was ready to return to the big leagues.

This time he was loaded for bear. Stevens won with a more-than-respectable fifteen percent of his mounts that year and an impressive twenty percent of his graded stakes horses. With Tsunami Slew, he won the Carleton F. Burke Handicap at Santa Anita, Eddie Read Handicap at Del Mar, and American Handicap at Hollywood Park. When D. Wayne Lukas took McHargue off Tank's Prospect for the Arkansas Derby, a $500,000 race, he tapped Stevens. It was the first time the rider had traveled out of California for a big race. He won in Arkansas and had his first Kentucky Derby mount.

Kentucky Derby glory eluded him that year, but not for long. The missing ingredient from his early years, confidence, had since been infused in Stevens by his success in riding winners in California and by the affirmation that trainers like Lukas were riding him. By 1988 he was sure of himself. "I felt I could ride with anybody, that there was no one better than me. It wasn't a question of if I was going to win a Kentucky Derby; it was when. That was my mental approach to everything — very positive. I'd ridden some grade I winners, and Lukas had started to use me on a regular basis."

Stevens got aboard the Lukas-trained and Gene Klein-owned filly Winning Colors to win the Santa Anita Oaks in March of 1988. She was so impressive that the connections wheeled her back a month later against the boys in the Santa Anita Derby, another tour de force. There was no doubt her next start would be in Louisville the first Saturday in May, but for a moment there was some doubt who would ride her.

"Within a day of her Santa Anita Derby, Cordero tried to get the mount on her because he'd had success with Wayne," Stevens said, "and McCarron and all of them were trying to get me off her. It's the same old thing: 'He's never won the big dance before and I've done it.' At that time I wasn't a big-race rider, and knowing what I know now, Wayne could have justifiably taken me off. But he and Mr. Klein chose not to. They had the utmost confidence in me.

"When Wayne legged me up for the Derby, he patted me on the thigh and said, 'Go have a good time. Enjoy this.' Those were his instructions, and I was going to get the job done."

The job got done by gaining a clear-cut advantage at every call after leaving from post eleven. With a half-mile of running left Winning Colors cleared off by four lengths and needed each one of them to hold off the strong charge of Forty Niner and Pat Day down the stretch. The winning margin was a neck, and Stevens was credited with a masterful ride, building just enough cushion to get the filly home. "When I'm in a battle the final sixteenth, something happens in me and second isn't good enough, and there's no way I'm going to get beat," Stevens said years later.

The ultimate praise came from Shoemaker, who said after the race, "He (Stevens) finishes strong and uses the whip well with either hand. He has a good head and his own style." Ironically, copied partly from Shoemaker himself.

Dave Johnson, the racing announcer who called that and many other Kentucky Derbys for ABC, remembers being amazed by Stevens' attitude after the race. "I went out to California to do a piece on Gary before the Preakness," Johnson said. "I asked him what he would have done if he'd lost the Derby. He replied, 'I couldn't have.' I answered that he could have stumbled, that anything could have happened. 'There was no way I could have lost the Derby,' he kept saying. His mindset was so incredibly positive; that's the kind of jockey I'd want riding my horse."

Stevens credits tactical planning for part of his success. Like McCarron, Pat Day, and Jerry Bailey, the other top "money" riders of his time, Stevens leaves nothing unturned when plotting out how he thinks a race will be run. "You think everything out, but never stick to one game plan," he said. "You have to adapt and improvise in a heartbeat, and change tactics if that's what needs to be done. I think my biggest asset, however, is my mental strength. I know when I walk on a racetrack there's no one better than me, no one can finish with me, and nobody can ride with me. I don't know if that's true or not, but that's how I prepare myself. When I go out on the racetrack, it's war. I don't have any friends. It goes back to when I was riding against my brother. On the track he wasn't my brother, and he damn sure wasn't my friend. And that's how I do it every day."

The fire that carried Stevens to the top also burned him, however. His temper was legendary, particularly in the early stages of his career. "I was a nightmare in my twenties, real fiery," Stevens admitted. "I would argue about anything, whether I was playing golf or skiing. I used to be a club-thrower on the golf course, and I'd fight at the drop of a hat in the jocks' room. I think my biggest weakness was my temper. I could never take criticism well, still don't. But I was too fiery back then. I know I'm a selfish person, and I'm basically married to what I do, riding."

His marriage to Toni Baze, the daughter of trainer Carl Baze, produced four children, but ended in divorce in 1995, a victim partially of that temperament that serves Stevens so well in his work. "I thrive on pressure, but my family and friends suffered from it because I used to be a nightmare in the days before a big race, and I wouldn't even realize it. Nobody wanted to be around me because I would become very selfish and self-centered and very focused on that one race, and I never realized it until the last five years. I'd realize I'd just acted like an ass, because of the pressure that was coming. But I thrive on it. I feel like I am always able to rise to another level in the big events because of what that pressure is doing for me. Fear of failure is a big part of it. I'd think the only way a certain horse could lose is if I screwed up."

Following the divorce, Stevens, though still competi-

Thunder Gulch gave Stevens Derby No. 2.

tive, mellowed a lot, began to relax more, and started to smell the roses. "I've learned to point the energy in a different direction," he said. He did some soul-searching and felt he wasn't happy with his life. Although his career continued to roll along, it began to feel stagnant, and he decided to take his show far down the road to Hong Kong and Europe. The well-spoken Stevens wowed them on and off the track in Europe and Asia.

"I found out when I went to Hong Kong that American racing is not well respected around the world. I had to fight for information on what was going on leading up to our Triple Crown races in 1995. Nobody cared. And in England we're considered newcomers on the block. Racing's been there for centuries, and they don't think we have any history here. Now I'm married to an English girl (Nikki), so I deal with it every day."

Stevens' time overseas gave him a fresh outlook, and he found a new appreciation of his life stateside. Before he'd left on his world tour, Stevens felt he could get by nicely abroad without riding the Triple Crown season. As that time got closer, however, he changed his mind. He began commuting between Hong Kong and Los Angeles, and rode the diminutive Larry the Legend to a stunning win in the 1995 Santa Anita Derby. When "Larry" got injured, Lukas stepped forward with Thunder Gulch after Mike Smith had taken off him. "We never had a straw in our path," Stevens said after winning the Kentucky Derby for the second time.

Things actually got better two years later. Stevens found out in the days leading up to the 1997 Derby that he'd been tabbed for induction into racing's Hall of Fame. Then he went out and partnered with the Bob Baffert-trained Silver

Charm, a charismatic gray colt who captured the imagination of the public, to gamely win the Derby once again. Silver Charm was all heart and threatened to become racing's first Triple Crown winner since Affirmed in 1978 after taking the Preakness. He was the kind of horse that seemingly wouldn't let anyone go by him during crunch time. In the Belmont Stakes, though, Silver Charm suffered a deflating defeat when Chris McCarron snuck by him close to home aboard Touch Gold, flying so far out in the middle of the track that Silver Charm didn't see him until it was too late.

"I was very emotional for three months after Silver Charm got beat in the Belmont," Stevens said, "but as far as feeling any animosity toward Chris or anything, that's what makes this sport. We're paid to go out there and do the best job that we can do, and if it would have been handed to us on a silver platter, it wouldn't have been nearly as enjoyable as if we had happened to have won on that day."

In a strange twist of fate, Stevens played the opposite role in the very next Belmont. In 1998 Baffert again had saddled the Derby and Preakness winner, Real Quiet, and hit New York for the second straight year with the Triple Crown tantalizingly within his grasp. When jockey Kent Desormeaux committed Real Quiet to the front end over the sweeping Belmont layout, the race was on. Stevens, riding Victory Gallop for Prestonwood Farm and trainer Elliott Walden, rallied from the clouds to deny Real Quiet the glory by an agonizing nose.

"I knew in my heart I was the only one who could beat Real Quiet going into that race," said Stevens. "At the eighth pole I didn't think I was going to get there, and at the sixteenth pole I thought there was a slim shot." The horses bumped coming down the lane, which might well have led to Real Quiet's disqualification had he gotten to the wire first. But the nose on the line was that of Stevens' mount.

"It was bittersweet," he said. "I think everyone down deep hopes there'll be a Triple Crown winner. But if you can be the spoiler, that's what you want to be. And if you couldn't be the spoiler, then you're rooting for the Triple Crown. But anyone in the jocks' room who said they didn't care if they won the race or not, they're liars."

A year and a half after the Victory Gallop triumph, and the month after winning the Juvenile with Anees, Stevens climbed off Desert Hero after the Malibu and told trainer Richard Mandella that he'd just ridden his last race. The pain in his knees, aggravated by a string of injuries throughout Stevens' career, had become all-consuming. The degenerative arthritis made it difficult for him to concentrate on his riding. A couple of days after announcing his retirement at the end of 1999, Stevens said the pain had started in 1985 with his first bad knee injury and had worsened considerably in the past year.

"People say, 'well, other people play with pain,'" he said at the time. "I've played with pain for twenty-one years. Usually it means you're injured but eventually it's going to get better. With the knees, they were never getting better. Always worse. I quit because I couldn't compete at the same level I've been used to for twenty-one years. Every day I rode I felt the confidence slipping away, and I didn't feel I was as good a rider as I was twelve months ago. I tried changing stirrups and moving this and moving that, and I was still hurting. Going down the backside in races I'd be thinking 'Man, this hurts' instead of 'that's a great spot right there, I'm gonna get up here on the rail and sit.' It wasn't clicking anymore."

The pain-killing injections, the continuous racing calendar, knee operations through the years, and the normal wear and tear had all caught up. For a man of his success, Stevens looked a tragic figure on the patio of his foothills home above Santa Anita days after his retirement. "It's 12:30 now," he said wistfully, "and I should have been in the jocks' room two hours ago. Go into the sauna, play a couple of games of Chinese checkers, have a nice hot shave, relax, go over the *Form* again, make any mental changes. That's all I've done for a long time. That's where my body's clock is telling me I should be."

After mulling over various offers, Stevens decided that television work, which he'd handled with skill in previous years when injured, would not give him much chance to be around horses and still be part of the sights, smells, and sounds of the racetrack. He took a job as assistant trainer to Alex Hassinger, who was training privately for The Thoroughbred Corp., for which Stevens had been riding first call. Within the next few months Stevens got his trainer's license and began picking up the subtleties of horses that are often taken for granted. The trainer's son was learning his father's trade, but there seemed always a sense that Stevens was somehow out of his element.

While getting satisfaction out of training, the excitement didn't come every day. There was nowhere to release that pressure. And there was being on call twenty-four hours a day and the constantly changing plans of each horse and making sure all bases were covered. He would get on horses occasionally, with mixed results.

Then, six months into retirement, he began noticing a

big difference in the way the more painful of his knees reacted to simple things and chores around the house. "I had begun taking a glucosamine and chondroitin product immediately after retiring," said Stevens. "That and walking and the time off, basically that was it. The knee began feeling a lot better." Stevens decided to have another go at riding. He waited for a lump sum payout from an insurance company for his disability, knowing that when he came back to riding, he likely would not be able to insure his knees again. But as he galloped more horses and realized the pain had subsided, there was no doubt his retirement was about to be retired.

"I tested my knee hard in the mornings; it held up well, and I was very fit. I had no question in my mind I was coming back a lot better than I'd been the year before I retired," he said. Stevens was back in the saddle for the October 4 opening of Santa Anita's Oak Tree meeting, not setting the world on fire, but riding well enough. He may have been convinced he was fine, but others needed to be shown.

The proof came one month later in the 2000 Breeders' Cup Mile, run at Churchill Downs. War Chant was a talented and top-bred colt who had recently been switched to the turf. Stevens kept him well back in the early stages and then unleashed a run from seemingly too far back. But War Chant chewed up the scenery and got up to win in a powerful performance. Stevens knew the significance of the victory. "It was probably one of my most satisfying moments because it proved to the whole racing world that I was back. That was one of the better rides and finishes of my career. I told people that this wasn't an attempted comeback, this was a comeback."

Lightning nearly struck twice that day, as Stevens made another hellacious charge from way back in the Juvenile, aboard a strapping colt named Point Given. This time, the rider missed by the scantiest of noses. Tempering that defeat was the knowledge that he had a significant Triple Crown horse for the following spring.

That winter took a cold and dark turn, however. Stevens attempted to intervene in the life of his fellow rider and friend, Chris Antley, who had spiraled down a tube of depression, alcohol, and drugs. Stevens found in a visit to Antley's home that he couldn't connect with him, couldn't pull him out of his mania. A few weeks later, on December 3, Antley was found dead. Stevens was shaken, and he criticized the police investigation and coroner's report, which ruled out homicide.

Two weeks after Antley's death, Stevens found an unrelated threatening note in his locker seeking to extort money from him. The writers claimed to have proof that Stevens passed an electrical device to Pat Day after the 1995 Kentucky Derby, an old accusation that had come to nothing. After contacting authorities, Stevens left two packages for the extortionists, who were arrested after leading police to their home.

After that kind of winter the Triple Crown trail must have looked like paradise to Stevens. Teaming with familiars Baffert and The Thoroughbred Corp., Stevens was on a mountain of horse in the 2001 Santa Anita Derby. Point Given had grown and filled out to 1,200 pounds. Anyone who watched him toy with his field that day felt the same: Here was your Kentucky Derby winner. Here was, finally, the Triple Crown winner.

In Louisville, Point Given picked a bad day to run a bad

race. Why he faltered as the Derby favorite became much debated. The Churchill Downs strip was ultrafast that day, with decent horses setting track records all day long. Perhaps it was packed down too hard, too jarring for the heavyweight colt. Stevens' decision to ride just as he did at

SKIP DICKSTEIN

In 2001 Stevens and Point Given dominated.

Santa Anita, close to the pace, was questioned in retrospect. He seemed in a good spot, but was the pace too hot? As good as everyone thought Point Given was, this shouldn't have even mattered. But it's horse racing, and they do get beat.

It's just harder to take when the horse comes back in the Preakness and Belmont Stakes looking like Superman again. Another near-miss in the Triple Crown, with a twist. Whatever happened to Point Given in the Derby was proven a fluke when he went on to win the Haskell and Travers that summer, Stevens aboard. Before the Haskell, when Baffert tried to relay last-second advice to the rider through an outrider, however, Stevens was not amused. It was an insult to him, and his horse became agitated by the outrider as well. After the race Stevens and Baffert engaged in an X-rated conversation, and there was no smile from the rider in the winner's circle photos.

As the racing world salivated at the thought of Point Given taking on his elders in what promised to be a bang-up Breeders' Cup Classic, the Thunder Gulch colt was found to have exited his Travers triumph with a strained tendon in his left foreleg. He was retired at the end of August 2001. Stevens, ironically, partnered with Macho Uno to run fourth in the Breeders' Cup Classic. Macho Uno was the horse who had beaten Point Given by a nose in the previous year's Breeders' Cup Juvenile.

Through the dark moments, however, the sun shines once again on Stevens, a warrior in need of a good war to wage. He looks back on the Silver Charms, Winning Colors, and Serena's Songs fondly, but is much happier in the present, still with big horses, every day climbing aboard to do battle. The knees are holding up well so far, and the flame, well, that was never in question.

"I've always worn my heart on my sleeve, and I will continue to do that until the day I die," Stevens said. "I began having to prove myself when I was trying to keep on a level with my brothers, and always trying to make Dad proud. I guess I'm just competitive by nature."

PATRICK VALENZUELA

A Lifetime of Chance

"This is my last chance," the troubled rider said upon returning to racing after a suspension. "I know that. I am sure of it. There is no doubt of it. I am going to do exactly what is asked of me. I will attend substance-abuse meetings five times a week if requested. I have the support of trainers and other jockeys. When I rode out for the first race, some folks in the grandstand had a banner that said, 'Welcome Back Pat.' "

Patrick Valenzuela spoke the preceding words "with obvious sincerity," according to the reporter who included them in his story of the rider's comeback after the enforced absence. The problem for Valenzuela, however, is that it's anyone's guess when the quote is from — he's spoken similar words in 1989, 1991, 1993, 1997, 1999, and 2001. It's not the kind of multiple-choice test Valenzuela, or anyone else, wants to take (the correct answer is 1991). We're supposed to learn from our mistakes and move on.

But the demons rage hard inside Valenzuela. Recovering addicts slip, but to the public it sometimes seems Valenzuela is living in a banana-peel factory. Nobody argues that he could have been one of the all-time great riders. He has the natural ability, a way with horses, and the pedigree. But in a career that spans more than twenty years, the rider has managed to squeeze about twelve productive ones between eight stewards' suspensions and a host of personal problems.

It wasn't supposed to be this way for Patrick Valenzuela, who was born in 1962 in Montrose, Colorado, in the Rockies. He was bred for racing, the son of a jockey, A.C. Valenzuela, and the nephew of four other riders, including Ismael "Milo" Valenzuela, who twice won the Kentucky Derby and Preakness. Pat's brother, Fabian, rode in Arizona and California, and his cousin, Fernando Valenzuela, is a journeyman. Pat grew up with horses from the time he was knee-high, and riding is all he ever thought about doing.

"When I was seven, I'd get up on Saturday mornings and go to the track, and I'd be walking down the shed rows and here'd come Bill Shoemaker," he remembered. "My dad would tell me to 'squat down and show Mr. Shoemaker how you're gonna ride when you get older.' And I'd squat down and act like I was riding."

At sixteen Valenzuela was already competing against the legend and sending relatives win pictures of himself besting Shoemaker. "My brother sent Pat to me a couple of years before he started riding," Milo Valenzuela said. "You could see right away that he could ride. He was eager to learn. The only thing I did was help polish him a little bit." Milo Valenzuela rode Tim Tam in 1958 and Forward Pass ten years later. Both Calumet Farm runners won the Kentucky Derby and Preakness only to finish second in the Belmont Stakes.

Sixteen is still a tender age, though, too tender to be out

on one's own without a good education, making money before establishing a solid foundation. Valenzuela ended up with the wrong kind of early education from the wrong people, and an early introduction to drugs.

His breakthrough year as a rider occurred in 1980 as the seventeen-year-old became the youngest jockey to win the Santa Anita Derby when he scored aboard Codex. Great Lady M. and Ack's Secret became multiple stakes winners for Valenzuela that year, during which time Patrick won 234 races. The following year Valenzuela won the Wilshire Handicap, the Beverly Hills Handicap, and the Vanity Handicap, all in less than two months, and all aboard the filly Track Robbery. The following year, he again rode the filly to a stakes win, in the Spinster at Keeneland. Not once in those four races, said Valenzuela, did he ever lay a stick on her.

Highlights like those should have been regular occurrences for Valenzuela, but nothing in his life has quite turned out according to plan. Those who wonder how he has continued to receive chances through the years and decades, however, have likely never met the man. For if his meandering life holds any constants, they are these: Patrick Valenzuela is extremely likable; and he can ride racehorses.

He possesses a quick smile in the best and worst of times. His manner is easy, his conversation engaging, a laugh at the ready. He is animated, with unbridled enthusiasm whenever he launches into a story. His memory is incredible when it comes to horses and races and points within races. Those race-replay kiosks at racetracks today have nothing over Valenzuela. He is also quick to accept the blame coming to him. All of this, plus his history in Southern California racing and a string of good attorneys, goes a long way in explaining why he has received so many chances to clean up and ride. But it makes his continuing failure to do so consistently all the more frustrating for his friends and clients.

His horsemanship has never been questioned. He earned a reputation for getting speed horses to break brilliantly from the gate and never look back. Horsemen such as Charles Whittingham and Mel Stute enjoyed enormous success with him. Pat Valenzuela has that special talent among riders, the one that makes even his detractors admit horses just seem to run for him.

"It has to do with feelings, tone of voice, horsemanship, and physical ability," Valenzuela explained. "The horse is doing most of the work, so the jockey has to adapt to the

Valenzuela after his Santa Anita Derby victory on
Sunday Silence.

horse's ability to run. It doesn't work if you try to get the horse to perform to the best of your ability. We have to get that horse to perform to his best — become one with him like a machine.

"You have to get along with him, give the horse the confidence he needs, and instill in him a confidence in you. When that happens and you're coming down the stretch and everything's hitting on all cylinders and you get that extra gear — it's a feeling you can't even believe."

Valenzuela posted steady if not spectacular numbers throughout most of the 1980s, and each year he seemed to have a big horse. In 1984 it was Interco, winner of three grade I races at Santa Anita during the winter/spring meeting, the San Fernando, the Big 'Cap, and the San Luis Rey. One year later, the three-year-old filly Fran's Valentine stormed home in the Las Virgenes, the Santa Susana, the Kentucky Oaks, and the Yankee Valor Handicap for Valenzuela. Fran's Valentine, trained by Joe Manzi, had gotten home first in the inaugural running of the Breeders' Cup Juvenile Fillies in 1984 under Valenzuela at nearly 75-1, only to be disqualified and placed tenth for interference.

In 1986 two-year-old filly Brave Raj and Valenzuela went on a run, taking down the Sorrento Stakes at Del Mar before winning two legs of the Florida Stallion Stakes. Two years after the Breeders' Cup disappointment of Fran's Valentine, Valenzuela won the Juvenile Fillies for trainer Mel Stute by five and a half lengths with Brave Raj, the daughter of Rajab. With that win Brave Raj became the richest two-year-old filly in history and earned an Eclipse Award as divisional champion.

Very Subtle was Valenzuela's next big winner, taking Saratoga's Test Stakes in 1987 before trying the Breeders'

Cup Sprint at Hollywood Park. The three-year-old daughter of Hoist the Silver, also conditioned by Stute, was dismissed at 16-1 that day. Valenzuela alertly gunned her to the front in the field of thirteen, and she widened the rest of the way, winning by four lengths over Groovy, who suffered his first defeat of the year but went on to be named champion sprinter for 1987.

Early in 1989 Whittingham was trying to prepare a three-year-old campaign for a bad-acting colt by Halo, himself known as a nasty horse who even years later as a stud had to be muzzled to protect horses and people in his vicinity. The black colt in Whittingham's barn had deposited Shoemaker on the ground rather than go work one morning, so Whittingham gave Valenzuela the call on him. Sunday Silence captured the San Felipe that March and wheeled right back to claim the Santa Anita Derby three weeks later. This set up a geographic rivalry between Sunday Silence and the scourge of the East, the Ogden Phipps-owned Easy Goer.

While not quite Alydar and Affirmed, they were clearly the two best of their crop, but Easy Goer, riding the Eastern bias, was sent off at eighty cents on the dollar in the Kentucky Derby, with Valenzuela and Sunday Silence a tick over 3-1. After an eventful trip in which he broke into another horse, had to be steadied after a separate incident, and then swerved down the lane, Sunday Silence won handily by two and a half lengths over Easy Goer.

Valenzuela could remember watching his uncle and Forward Pass in the Derby, and now he, too, had climbed to the top of the racing world. "I was six years old watching on television with my family," he said, "and I always wondered what that last quarter-mile must feel like. Now I know. The stretch is like a tunnel you're running through where there's nothing but noise." Valenzuela took his place among the California jockeys who had won the previous three runnings of the race, Gary Stevens, Chris McCarron, and Shoemaker. "Pat is a good kid," said Laffit Pincay Jr., who rode pacesetter Houston in Sunday Silence's Derby. "He's got a good heart and everyone likes him. He has overcome personal problems and winning the Derby is going to help him."

If you believe in foreshadowing, however, the winner's circle ceremony after the Derby provided omens that Valenzuela's future might not be a smooth ride. Kentucky's then-governor, Wallace Wilkinson, referred to him as "Pat Velasquez," and commentator Jim McKay dropped the jockey's trophy. "It doesn't bother me as long as they make out the check to me, give me the trophy, and put my name in the record books," Valenzuela joked afterward.

It was the rematch between Sunday Silence and Easy Goer in the Preakness that cemented Valenzuela in the lore of racing. The public still was not sold on the West Coast hero after the Derby, and Easy Goer actually went off at shorter odds, .60-1, than he had two weeks earlier. This time Pat Day got the early jump aboard the favorite, making a move up the backstretch while shutting Sunday Silence off to the inside. Day acknowledged that with Sunday Silence behind him, he thought he could give his colt a breather before asking for his closing kick. Before he knew it, however, Sunday Silence was on even terms around the turn, and to his outside.

They remained locked together, Easy Goer running hard up against the rail and Sunday Silence so close to his outside Day could do little with the whip in his right hand. They raced as one all the way home, stuck so tightly that

Day laid a claim of foul against Valenzuela, which was subsequently dismissed. "I thought maybe his horse shifted out, my horse drifted in a little, but neither horse missed a step," said Valenzuela. "Our boots might have brushed, but we didn't make contact. I was hitting Sunday Silence on the left shoulder down the lane because there wasn't room to hit him on the hindquarters. I switched to my right hand, and he really picked it up the last sixteenth. The last five jumps we had the momentum, so I knew I'd won it."

The margin was just a nose, but Valenzuela had indeed won it, out-riding one of the top jockeys in the world in the process. Although Easy Goer was able to deny Sunday Silence the Triple Crown with a decisive victory on his home court at Belmont Park, Valenzuela's reputation was made.

Another reputation was creeping over the horizon and into his world, however. With the three-year-old championship and Horse of the Year title up for grabs in the Breeders' Cup Classic that November, the duel between Easy Goer and Sunday Silence was about to reach its pinnacle. One of the principals wasn't at Gulfstream Park that day, though. In October Valenzuela called in sick several times and the Santa Anita stewards requested he be drug tested, nothing new at that time for the rider. Getting a positive for cocaine, Valenzuela was handed a sixty-day suspension October 27.

Valenzuela watched with the rest of the racing world as Sunday Silence defeated Easy Goer once again in the Breeders' Cup, this time by a neck under Chris McCarron. More than a decade later, Valenzuela can hardly believe it. "I took off some of the biggest races in the world for a little white powder," he said. "I didn't give myself a fair shake, and I didn't give the horsemen a fair shake."

Valenzuela had done enough good riding, however, to attract the attention of jet magnate Allen Paulson, a California-based owner and breeder who had invested heavily in top stock and seemed to race all of it in the Breeders' Cup. He signed Valenzuela on as his contract rider, and Patrick didn't disappoint — at first. In the 1991 Breeders' Cup Mile at Churchill Downs, Valenzuela rated Opening Verse, a son of The Minstrel, behind the leaders in the fourteen-horse field. Gaining room to angle out in upper stretch, they drifted out in the final furlong but did so with speed, beating Val des Bois by better than a length at 26-1.

That same afternoon, Valenzuela was aboard for one of the most memorable Breeders' Cup contests, the Juvenile,

Valenzuela piloted Arazi to a stunning victory in the Breeders' Cup Juvenile.

245

in which he rode Arazi, a Paulson-owned son of Blushing Groom shipped from France. After breaking slowly, Arazi began a charge from thirteenth place that electrifies viewers to this day. Arazi turned the Juvenile into his own match race, winning by five lengths while being taken in hand the last seventy yards. Valenzuela was winning them every which way on every kind of horse, and he was flying high.

Valenzuela tells you tales of his biggest wins with his hands clutching at imaginary reins, his chair doubling as a strapping Thoroughbred, and his voice rising as he relives in-race conversations with his horse and fellow jockeys. Paulson had invited him to his house before the 1992 Breeders' Cup races at Gulfstream Park, impressing the jockey with his state-of-the-art video system and with the promise that if Patrick could win all four Breeders' Cup races he was riding for the owner and/or his wife, Madeleine, his bonus would be a Rolls Royce.

He knocked off the Juvenile Fillies without incident when Eliza won for fun. "She was just dragging me around there," the rider said. "I'm thinking, 'here comes the Rolls.' But Fowda was trying to get out on me in the Distaff and didn't run well. Then Arazi — I had him in good striking position in the Mile — but he'd had surgery and just didn't turn out to be the horse we thought he'd be.

"But Fraise came out of the gate nice and easy in the Turf. We broke last and I went over and sat on the hedge. You can push the hedge over a little at Gulfstream and make more room. At the five-eighths I'm about ten lengths off them and I'm thinking, 'I can win this race.' Pat Day makes the lead on Sky Classic and he's watching his back. But I shoot by at the hedge making this bold move, and I'm up alongside him at the sixteenth pole. Pat looks over and does a double-take and gets to riding, but I have the jump on him. I nosed him at the wire. I ended up getting a Lexus from Mr. Paulson for the two wins."

Just a couple of weeks after getting the car, Valenzuela was driving behind a flatbed truck that suddenly lost an axle. The jockey swerved to avoid the vehicle, but clipped the rear of the truck. Valenzuela was saved by the airbag; the Lexus was demolished. The following March, Valenzuela's contract to ride for Paulson was destroyed as well. The contract, worth a reported one million dollars including incentives, ran out at the end of 1992, but was being renewed by a series of one-month, handshake agreements. But Valenzuela missed a swath of the Santa Anita season with a back injury, a virus, and the omnipresent personal problems. McCarron had stepped in again, riding Corby to victory in the San Felipe Stakes for Paulson, who decided that committing to one jockey, especially the mercurial Valenzuela, was too restrictive.

Fraise would be Valenzuela's sixth, and thus far, last, Breeders' Cup winner. The rider's long downward spiral through drug abuse, domestic difficulties (he is divorced, with four daughters), unexcused absences, and suspensions would continue for the balance of the nineties. Regardless of his accomplishments, plus any that may yet come, Valenzuela will always be known in horse racing as Mike Tyson is in boxing and Darryl Strawberry and Steve Howe are in baseball — talented individuals who tossed aside their gifts for reasons few "normies" (the recovering addict's parlance for outsiders) will understand. And continued to do so despite numerous chances to regain what they'd lost amid the catcalls and jeers of a skeptical public.

After failing to show up for opening day at Del Mar in

1995, Valenzuela was suspended for the meeting. He test-ed cleanly for drugs that time, but cited "family problems" for his absence. Two years later he was arrested by police in Arcadia on charges of spousal abuse. He had been sus-pended indefinitely by Santa Anita Park stewards for unex-cused absences the same week. Two years after that, Valenzuela, then thirty-six, was charged with robbing a cab driver of $150 at gunpoint. He was subsequently cleared of that charge. Amid all that, Valenzuela, while on his way to dinner in Pasadena one night, saw flames com-ing out of a mobile home and pulled a child out minutes before the home exploded.

By the mid-nineties Valenzuela's career was in tatters. He last achieved one hundred wins in 1994, slipping to eighty-three the next year and just seventy in 1996. He won exactly three races from sixty-two starts in 1997 and didn't ride at all in 1998 or for most of 1999, when he took part in a drug abuse recovery program through the Winners Foundation, a backstretch organization dedicated to help-ing employees with drug and alcohol problems. He was given a one-year conditional license to ride before the Oak Tree meeting that fall, revocable if he discontinued his par-ticipation with the Winners Foundation or refused to undergo random drug or alcohol testing.

Valenzuela talked at length at that time about his new-found spirituality, his embracing of Jesus Christ, and the turning around of his life. "Being in jail made me realize my four daughters could be taken away from me," he said. "It really opened my eyes to what would happen if I kept going down the road I was on. I'm in a position now where I can't rub two nickels together. But I've got spirituality and I've got serenity and sobriety and I've got my family behind me and my friends from the Winners Foundation. Today I can look you straight in the eye and tell you I'm a different person. And it's okay if I don't win another race because today I'm the Pat Valenzuela I'm supposed to be."

Prominent owners supported Valenzuela as he prepared to return to the races. Robert Lewis defended him passionately. Mike Pegram and Marty Wygod lined up behind him. And John and Betty Mabee, for whom Valenzuela had won several big races aboard Best Pal, including the inaugural Pacific Classic, voiced support.

Valenzuela began slowly at Oak Tree, but when racing moved to Hollywood Park for its two-month fall meeting, Valenzuela caught the old magic. This was the same meeting in which Laffit Pincay Jr. broke Shoemaker's all-time win record, and the Panamanian was on fire, getting top mounts every day. But Valenzuela chased him every step of the way for the riding title, eventually finishing second with twenty-eight winners to Pincay's thirty-two.

The circuit moved back to Santa Anita for its main 2000 meeting. Valenzuela had a slow first month of the meet and was in the middle of the riders' pack when he took off his mounts February 4 because of a neck injury. The following day, he was drug tested by the California Horse Racing Board for the first time since his relicensing. He admitted taking amphetamines and was suspended with the recommendation he not be relicensed until he could prove one year of uninterrupted sobriety. Two months after being suspended, he was asked what had happened.

"Basically I slipped out of my sobriety," he said. "It shocked the hell out of me that I chose to do drugs because I had my Christianity and my sobriety going for me. I thought there was no way I could use again. I just didn't have the right defenses for my addictive behavior. It had nothing to do with riding. There were expectations in my personal life, some things going on that I didn't like, and instead of talking to somebody about it, I chose the wrong thing to do."

The addict measures progress in baby steps, and Valenzuela is well versed in the language of twelve-step programs. He says he will be a recovering addict the rest of his life. Intellectually, he knows what he must do. And the small things provide solace. "I think I shocked the board by walking in there and admitting I'd used. That's a big difference from the past — running away for a week and coming back and lying abut being clean. Back then you couldn't get a hold of me with a search warrant. In the past I might have gone out and used over the suspension. But today I'm able to accept their decision. I may not like it, but I don't have to be verbal, get vulgar, be stupid, and take it out on anybody. That's a different Patrick today."

Just before Valenzuela was handed down this latest suspension, his fellow rider, Chris Antley, was found dead. Drugs were thought to have played a part in his demise. Although they weren't friends, Antley's death caught Valenzuela's attention. "It could have easily happened to me.

"People think athletes have it so much easier, but we're in the limelight, and your personal life and problems show up in the paper and the world reads about it and says 'how can this guy, who has the world on a string, how can he let this get in his life?' But we're only human, and we get caught up in the wrong things. We all have problems in life. When I was sixteen and I came out here, I was just working my ass off to become a jockey because I loved horse racing. I didn't know what cocaine or methamphetamines were. Then you get involved with the wrong crowd."

Nearly two years after his latest suspension, Valenzuela returned to riding with the start of Santa Anita's winter/spring meet in December 2001.

As usual, Valenzuela received a warm welcome on his first trip from the paddock to the racetrack. And he marked up his first winner on the final day of 2001. Hopefully that bodes well for the months and years to come. Now his future in racing is in the hands of the owners and trainers to whom he must sell his sobriety and his ability to win. Perhaps he will seize the opportunity and prove that he can still do what he was born and raised to do.

"Maybe they'll use me or maybe there will be resentment," he acknowledged. "All I know is when I'm on the back of a horse, you're going to see a jockey who's going to try and make a difference and get that horse to perform. That's the gift I've been given. I know I'll get back to the Derby sooner or later."

Perhaps Valenzuela still has another chapter or two he can write in the annals of horse racing history. When he appeared before the stewards at Santa Anita and got his license pulled in 2000, Valenzuela's hearing took place in a room where a bronze statue of Sunday Silence is prominently displayed. Valenzuela could not tell if it was he or McCarron depicted on the horse's back. It wasn't supposed to be this way.

About the Author

L enny Shulman has been a professional writer since age fifteen, when he began writing sports stories for his hometown newspaper, the *Westbury* (N.Y.) *Times*. He received a bachelor's degree in journalism from Syracuse University's Newhouse School of Communications and worked as assistant sports editor at the *Oneida* (N.Y.) *Daily Dispatch*.

Moving West, he served as editor for the *Tucson Night Times*, an arts and entertainment weekly, for three years. After moving to Los Angeles he began a television- and film-writing career. He was an Emmy-nominated writer/producer on the long-running show *Kids Incorporated*. He also wrote several HBO comedy specials and the feature film *Dice Rules*.

Returning to the world of sports, he won an Emmy Award in 1995 as writer/producer of FOX Sports' NFL Primetime Special. He began covering California racing for *The Blood-Horse* in 1998 before accepting the position as features editor for the magazine two years later. He lives in Kentucky with his family of Labrador Retrievers.

Other Titles *from*
ECLIPSE PRESS

At the Wire
Horse Racing's Greatest Moments

Baffert
Dirt Road to the Derby

Cigar
America's Horse (revised edition)

Country Life Diary
(revised edition)

Crown Jewels of Thoroughbred Racing

Dynasties
Great Thoroughbred Stallions

Etched in Stone

Four Seasons of Racing

Great Horse Racing Mysteries

Hoofprints in the Sand
Wild Horses of the Atlantic Coast

Horse Racing's Holy Grail
The Epic Quest for the Kentucky Derby

Investing in Thoroughbreds
Strategies for Success

Lightning in a Jar
Catching Racing Fever

Matriarchs
Great Mares of the 20th Century

Olympic Equestrian

Royal Blood

Thoroughbred Champions
Top 100 Racehorses of the 20th Century

Women in Racing
In Their Own Words

THOROUGHBRED
Legends®
S E R I E S

Affirmed and Alydar

Citation

Dr. Fager

Forego

Go for Wand

John Henry

Man o' War

Nashua

Native Dancer

Personal Ensign

Ruffian

Seattle Slew

Spectacular Bid

Sunday Silence

Swaps

A Division of The Blood-Horse, Inc.
PUBLISHERS SINCE 1916